BUCKINGHA

A GENEALOGICAL
BIBLIOGRAPHY

— BY —
STUART A. RAYMOND

FEDERATION OF FAMILY HISTORY SOCIETIES

10 664 5069

Published by the
Federation of Family History Societies,
c/o The Benson Room, Birmingham & Midland Institute,
Margaret Street, Birmingham, B3 3BS, U.K.

Copies also available from:
S.A. & M.J. Raymond, 6 Russet Avenue, Exeter, Devon, EX1 3QB, U.K.

Text processed and printed by
Oxuniprint, Oxford University Press

Cataloguing in publication data:

RAYMOND, Stuart A., 1945- .
Buckinghamshire: a genealogical bibliography. British genealogical
bibliographies. Birmingham, England: Federation of Family History Societies,
1993.

DDC: 016.9291094259

ISBN: 1 872094 72 4

ISSN: 1033-2065

CONTENTS

INTRODUCTION

This bibliography is intended primarily for genealogists. It is, however, hoped that it will also prove useful to historians, librarians, archivists, research students, and anyone else interested in Buckinghamshire history and families. It is intended to be used in conjunction with my *English genealogy: an introductory bibliography*, and the other titles in the *British genealogical bibliographies* series. A full list of these titles is given on the back cover.

Many genealogists, when they begin their research, fail to realise just how much information has been published, and is readily available in printed form. Not infrequently, they head straight for the archives, when they would probably do best to check printed sources first. When faced with the vast array of tomes possessed by major reference libraries, they do not know where to begin. This bibliography, in conjunction with the others in the series, is intended to help you find that beginning, and to provide guidance in following through the quest for ancestors. My aim has been to list everything relating to Buckinghamshire that has been published, and is likely to be of use to genealogists. In general, I have not included works which are national in scope, but which have local content. Such works may be identified in *English genealogy: an introductory bibliography*. I have also excluded the innumerable notes and queries found in such journals as *Origins*, except where the content is of importance. Where I have included such notes, replies to them are cited in the form 'see also', with no reference to the names of respondents. Local and church histories have also been excluded, except in a few cases. Such histories are frequently invaluable for genealogical purposes, but a full listing of them would require another volume. Newspaper articles are also excluded—although it is worth noting here that the *Bucks Advertiser* printed several transcripts of parish registers from the pen of R. Ussher in the first years of the century—including Buckingham, 1561-1796, Long Crendon, 1559-1837, Maids Moreton, 1558-1812, and Steeple Claydon, 1575-1812.

Be warned—I cannot claim that this bibliography is comprehensive. Neither do I claim that it is totally accurate. Most works cited I have seen—but not all. Some works have been deliberately excluded; others I have undoubtedly missed. If you come across anything I have missed, please let me know, so that it can be included in a second edition in due course.

Most works listed here are readily available in the libraries listed below—although no library holds everything. Even if you are overseas, you should be able to find copies of the more important reference works in larger research libraries. However, some items may prove difficult to locate—particularly articles in local periodicals. Never fear! Librarians believe in the doctrine of the universal availability of publications, and most public libraries are able to tap into the international inter-library loans system. Your local library should be able to borrow most of the items listed here, even if it has to go overseas to obtain them.

The work of compiling this bibliography has depended heavily on the libraries I have used. These included the British Library, the Local Studies Collection at Aylesbury, the Bodleian Library at Oxford, and the City and University libraries in Exeter. I am grateful to the librarians of these institutions for their help. Eve McLaughlin kindly provided details of her publications. I am also grateful to the Buckinghamshire Family History Society, and especially to Angela Hillier, Ray Shrimpton and Sue Allaby for their assistance. Alan Dell kindly read and commented on the first draft of this book; Brian Christmas proof-read it. My thanks to Jeremy Gibson, Bob Boyd, and to the officers of the Federation of Family History Societies, without whose support this series could not continue.

Stuart A. Raymond

LIBRARIES AND RECORD OFFICES

The major libraries and record offices concerned with Buckinghamshire history are:

Local Studies Collection
County Reference Library
County Library H.Q.
Walton Street
AYLESBURY
Bucks HP20 1UU

Buckinghamshire Archaeological Society
County Museum
Church Street
AYLESBURY
Bucks HP20 2QP

Buckinghamshire Record Office
County Hall
AYLESBURY
Bucks HP20 1UA

BIBLIOGRAPHIC PRESENTATION

Authors' names are in SMALL CAPITALS. Book and journal titles are in *italics*. Articles appearing in journals, and material such as parish register transcripts, forming only part of books are in inverted commas and textface type. Volume numbers are in **bold** and the individual number of the journal may be shown in parentheses. These are normally followed by the place of publication (except where this is London, which is omitted), the name of the publisher and the date of publication. In the case of articles, further figures indicate page numbers.

ABBREVIATIONS

B.A.S., R.B.	*Buckinghamshire Archaeological Society, Records Branch*
B.B.O.A.J.	*Berks, Bucks and Oxon Archaeological Journal*
B.F.H.S.	Buckinghamshire Family History Society
B.P.R.M.	*Buckinghamshire Parish Registers: Marriages*
B.P.R.S.	Buckinghamshire Parish Register Society
B.R.S.	Buckinghamshire Record Society
M.G.H.	*Miscellanea Genealogica et Heraldica*
O.	*Origins*
P.P.R.S.	*Phillimore's Parish Register Series*
R.o.B.	*Records of Buckinghamshire*

1. THE HISTORY OF BUCKINGHAMSHIRE

Genealogy is one of the historical sciences. In order to appreciate its significance, you need to read works which explain the context in which documents such as parish registers, tax lists, and probate records were created. You need an understanding of local history. The standard works on the history of Buckinghamshire are still:

LIPSCOMBE, GEORGE. *The history and antiquities of the County of Buckingham.* 4 vols. J. & W. Robins, 1847. This includes an extensive parochial survey, giving much information of genealogical value—manorial descents, lists of clergy, pedigrees, monumental inscriptions, etc., etc.

PAGE, WILLIAM, ed. *The Victoria History of the Counties of England: Buckinghamshire.* 4 vols, with index. Archibald Constable, et al, 1905-28. Contents: v.1. Domesday Book, Ecclesiastical history, etc. v.2. Social and Economic History, Schools, the three Hundreds of Aylesbury, etc. v.3. Aylesbury, Wendover, the three Hundreds of Chiltern, Cottesloe Hundred. v.4. Ashendon Hundred, Buckingham Hundred, Newport Hundred, Political History.

See also:

GIBBS, ROBERT. *Buckinghamshire: a record of local occurrences and general events, chronologically arranged.* 4 vols. Aylesbury: R. Gibbs, 1878-82. A chronological record of the county, noting many local events of potential genealogical interest.

GIBBS, ROBERT. *The Buckinghamshire miscellany: a series of concise and interesting articles illustrative of the history, topography and archaeology of the County of Buckingham.* Aylesbury: Bucks Advertiser & Aylesbury News, 1891.

SHEAHAN, JAMES JOSEPH. *History and topography of Buckinghamshire, comprising a general survey of the county* ... Longman Green Longman and Roberts, 1862. Parochial survey including lists of clergy, notes on manors and other property, etc.

A number of works covering areas smaller than the whole county provide parochial surveys similar to those found in the works of Sheahan and Lipscombe:

KENNETT, WHITE. *Parochial antiquities attempted in the history of Ambrosden, Burcester and other adjacent parts in the counties of Oxford and Bucks.* 2 vols. New ed. Oxford: Clarendon Press, 1818. Includes many charters. Mainly manorial descents.

GIBBS, ROBERT. *A history of Aylesbury with its borough and Hundreds, the hamlet of Walton, and the electoral division.* Aylesbury: Bucks Advertiser, 1885. Includes notes on the parish registers.

WILLIS, BROWNE. *The history and antiquities of the town, hundred and deanry of Buckingham* ... The author, 1755. Parochial survey of the Hundred including manorial descents, lists of clergy, monumental inscriptions, deed extracts from parish registers, etc., etc.

LANGLEY, THOMAS. *The history and antiquities of the Hundred and Deanery of Wycombe in Buckinghamshire, including the borough towns of Wycombe and Marlow, and sixteen parishes.* R. Faulder, et al, 1797. Includes manorial descents, monumental inscriptions, clergy lists, pedigrees (including folded pedigree of Borlam and Goodwin), etc., etc.

RATCLIFF, OLIVER. *History and antiquities of the Newport Pagnell Hundreds.* Olney: Cowper Press, 1900. Parochial survey, giving lists of clergy, manorial descents, some monumental inscriptions, etc.

Modern works tend to provide less information of genealogical value, but are of much more value to those wishing to understand their ancestors in the context of the society in which they lived. The following list is very much a personal selection, and is in rough chronological order. Those works which use genealogical sources for wider historical investigations will be of particular interest to you.

REED, MICHAEL A. *The Buckinghamshire landscape.* The making of the English landscape. Hodder and Stoughton, 1979.

ROYAL COMMISSION ON HISTORICAL MONUMENTS. *An inventory of the historical monuments in Buckinghamshire.* 2 vols. H.M.S.O., 1912-13. Includes brief note on important memorials.

CHIBNALL, A.C. *Beyond Sherington: the early history of the region of Buckinghamshire lying to the North-East of Newport Pagnell.* Phillimore, 1979. Medieval.

CORNWALL, J.C.K. 'Medieval peasant farmers', *R.o.B.* **20**, 1975-8, 57-75.

BLACK, W.H. 'On the personal names and surnames used in England in the thirteenth century', *Journal of the British Archaeological Association* **26**, 1870, 328-35. Names used in Hartwell and Stone.

RODEN, DAVID. 'Fragmentation of farms and fields in the Chiltern Hills, 13th century and later', *Mediaeval studies* **31**, 1969, 225-38. Based on manorial records.

REED, MICHAEL. 'Decline and recovery in a provincial urban network: Buckinghamshire towns, 1350-1800', in REED, MICHAEL, ed. *English towns in decline, 1350 to 1800.* Working papers **1**. Leicester: the University of Leicester Centre for Urban History, 1986. Unpaginated.

JORDAN, W.K. *The charities of rural England, 1480-1660: the aspirations and achievements of the rural society.* George Allen & Unwin, 1961. Based on wills of Buckinghamshire, Norfolk and Yorkshire.

REED, MICHAEL. 'Enclosure in North Buckinghamshire, 1500-1750', *Agricultural history review* **32**(2), 1984, 133-44.

HANLEY, H.A. 'Sixteenth century people: some aspects of social life in Elizabethan Bucks', *R.o.B.* **19**, 1971-4, 259-71.

CORNWALL, JULIAN. 'An Elizabethan census', *R.o.B.* **16**(4), 1959, 258-73.

HANLEY, H. 'Population mobility in Buckinghamshie, 1578-1583', *Local population studies* **15**, 1975, 33-9. Study of migration based on an Archdeaconry of Buckingham deposition book.

SKINNER, JOHN. 'Crisis mortality in Buckinghamshire, 1600-1750', *Local population studies* **28**, 1982, 67-72. Based on parish registers.

SKINNER, JOHN. 'Plague mortality in Buckinghamshire during the seventeenth century', *R.o.B.* **20**, 1975-8, 454-9. Based on parish registers.

PECK, LINDA LEVY. *Court patronage and corruption in early Stuart England.* Unwin Hyman, 1990. Includes a study of the patronage system in Buckinghamshire.

TURNER, M.E. 'Parliamentary enclosure and landownership change in Buckinghamshire', *Economic history review* 2nd series **28**, 1975, 565-81. Based on land tax records.

TURNER, MICHAEL. 'Parish landownership and the land tax assessments in twelve Buckinghamshire parishes: a comparison with enclosure awards', in TURNER, MICHAEL, & MILLS, DENNIS, eds. *Land and property: the English land tax 1692-1832.* Gloucester: Alan Sutton, 1986, 53-61.

TURNER, MICHAEL. 'Economic protest in rural society: opposition to parliamentary enclosure in Buckinghamshire', *Southern history* **10**, 1988, 94-128.

MORGAN, D.H. *Harvesters and harvesting: a study of the rural proletariat.* Croom Helm, 1982. Primarily concerned with Berkshire, Buckinghamshire and Oxfordshire.

BECKETT, I.F.W. 'The local community and the amateur military tradition: a case study of Victorian Buckinghamshire', *Journal of the Society for Army Historical Research* **59**, 1981, 95-110.

HORN, PAMELA. 'Child workers in the pillow lace and straw plait trades of Victorian Buckinghamshire and Bedfordshire', *Historical journal* **17**, 1974, 779-96.

MILLS, DENNIS, & MILLS, JOAN. 'Rural mobility in the Victorian censuses: experiences with a micro-computer program', *Local historian* **18**, 1988, 69-75. Based on the 1851 census for North Buckinghamshire and Lincolnshire.

WORKERS EDUCATIONAL ASSOCIATION (SLOUGH & ETON BRANCH) LOCAL HISTORY CLASS *A town in the making: Slough, 1851.* [ ]: Berkshire County Council. Town history based largely on 1851 census.

HORN, PAMELA L.R. 'The Buckinghamshire straw plait trade in Victorian England', *R.o.B.* **19**, 1971-4, 42-53.

HORN, C.A., & HORN, P. 'The social structure of an industrial community: Ivinghoe in Buckinghamshire in 1871', *Local Population Studies* **31**, 1983, 42-51.

BECKETT, I.F.W. 'The local community and the Great War: aspects of military participation', *R.o.B.* **20**, 1975-9, 503-15.

HORN, PAMELA. 'Agricultural trade unionism in Buckinghamshire, 1872-85', *R.o.B.* **20**, 1975-8, 76-86.

Local histories in general are excluded from this bibliography. However, a very select few are worth mentioning here, as representative of their genre.

Farnham Royal

CARR-GOMM, FRANCIS. *Records of the parish of Farnham Royal, Bucks, with an account of its church and parish registers, copies of ancient documents and monuments, and a full list of successive rectors.* Mitchell & Hughes, 1901. Includes 1821 enclosure award, some monumental inscriptions, list of churchwardens, pedigrees of Perryman and Umfreville and numerous extracts from original sources.

Milton Keynes

WOODFIELD, PAUL. *A guide to the historic buildings of Milton Keynes.* Milton Keynes: Milton Keynes Development Corporation, 1986. Brief descriptions with a few names of associated persons.

Sherington

CHIBNALL, A.C. *Sherington: fiefs and fields of a Buckinghamshire village.* Cambridge: C.U.P., 1965. Medieval-18th c. Traces the descent of the manor, and includes several lists of tenants, etc.

Stoke Mandeville

DELL, ALAN, & PEARCE, RICHARD. *Stoke Mandeville: where there's more crows than folk.* Chichester: Phillimore, 1992.

Diaries can be useful sources for genealogists. Buckinghamshire has had a number of prolific diarists who have named many people in their works. Three in particular stand out:

COLE, WILLIAM. *The Bletchley diary of the Rev. William Cole MA, FSA, 1765-67.* ed. Francis Griffin Stokes. Constable & Co., 1931.

MAYETT, JOSEPH. *The autobiography of Joseph Mayett of Quainton (1783-1839).* ed. Ann Kussmaul. B.R.S. **23**, 1986.

SPALDING, RUTH, ed. *The diary of Bulstrode Whitelocke, 1605-1675.* Records of Social and Economic History, N.S. **13**. Oxford: O.U.P., for the British Academy, 1990. Includes folded pedigree, 16-18th c., and innumerable references to contemporaries.

Not much has been published on emigration from Buckinghamshire. See, however:

McLAUGHLIN, EVE. 'Bound for Queensland', *O.* **12**(4), 1988, 31-2. Lists emigrants, 1847-74.

'So that's where Uncle Charlie went', *O.* **4**(3), 1980, 23-4. Index of Buckinghamshire emigrants with biographies in the *Cyclopedia of New Zealand.*

2. BIBLIOGRAPHY AND ARCHIVES

There is no modern published guide to the literature of Buckinghamshire history. Works of the nineteenth century and earlier are listed in:

GOUGH, H. *Bibliotheca Buckinghamiensis: a list of book relating to the County of Buckingham.* Aylesbury: G.T. De Fraine, 1890. Originally issued with *R.o.B.*

The present work is not the first attempt to list publications on Buckinghamshire genealogy. An earlier work, which may still be useful, is:

TOMLINSON, STEVEN. 'A genealogical bibliography for Oxfordshire, Berkshire and Buckinghamshire', *Oxfordshire Family Historian* **1**(5), 1978, 119-30. This lists a number of unpublished works and poll books excluded here.

The most important collection of published works on the county is at Aylesbury. It is described in two brief articles:

HARRIS, JULIE. 'The Buckinghamshire local collection', *O.* **3**(1), 1979, 22-4.

'Have you tried the library?', *O.* **12**(4), 1988, 12-14.

Once you have 'tried the library', you will need to visit archive repositories. A general discussion of the collections of Buckinghamshire County Record Office and Buckinghamshire Archaeological Society is provided in:

WOODMAN, A.V. 'Buckinghamshire records', *Genealogists' magazine* **11**(11), 1953, 371-7.

A useful general guide to sources of information, which includes a list of parish registers (now rather out of date) is:

Tracing your Buckinghamshire ancestors: a compendium of basic sources of information on Buckinghamshire inhabitants before 1837. Aylesbury: B.F.H.S., 1977.

For sources in the Milton Keynes area, consult:

McLAUGHLIN, EVE. 'North Bucks ancestors are an odd lot', *O.* **3**(1), 1979, 17-20.

The Buckinghamshire Record Office is the major archive repository in the county. A brief guide to its holdings for genealogists is:

BUCKINGHAMSHIRE RECORD OFFICE *Notes for the guidance of genealogists.* Aylesbury: Buckinghamshire County Council, 1987.

See also:

'After parish registers—what?', *O.* **4**(2), 1980, 13-14.

Buckinghamshire Record Office, 1938-1963: catalogue of an exhibition of records at the County Museum, Aylesbury, 24th June-20th July 1963. [Aylesbury: the Office, 1963.] Brief listing of documents exhibited.

It is worth combing through the lists of new accessions regularly published in:

BUCKINGHAMSHIRE RECORD OFFICE *Annual report and list of accessions.* [Aylesbury]: the Office, 1976- . There is also a *Consolidated index to list of accessions, 1976-1985.* 1988.

Extracts from these reports are regularly published in:

'County Record Office: extracts from the annual report by the County Archivist', *R.o.B.* **24**- , 1982- .

Accessions are also regularly reported in *O.*

Another important collection is that of the Buckinghamshire Archaeological Society. Accessions to its collections are regularly reported in 'Notes on recent accessions', *R.o.B.*, passim. This includes both manuscripts and printed books.

A number of works provide guidance for work on particular topics or sources at Buckinghamshire Record Office:

HANLEY, H.A. *House history: a short guide to sources.* Aylesbury: Buckinghamshire Record Office, 1987. See also *O.* **11**(4), 1987, 121-2. Brief general guide to a variety of records— tithe apportionments, inclosure awards, deeds, manorial and estate records, etc., etc.

CORNWALL, JULIAN C.K. 'The archives of the treasurers of Buckinghamshire before 1889', *Journal of the Society of Archivists* **1**(3), 1956, 70-74. General description of account and rate books.

CHARLTON, S.E. *Wartime Buckinghamshire, 1939-45: a brief guidee to sources.* [Aylesbury]: Buckinghamshire Record Office, 1992. Guide to sources on topics such as active service, evacuation, everyday life, etc., etc.

Ecclesiastical records are of major interest to genealogists. The major court for Buckinghamshire was that of the Archdeaconry of Buckingham. Its records are now in the Buckinghamshire Record Office, and are described in:

'Records of the Archdeaconry of Buckingham', *R.o.B.* **16**(4), 1959, 297-8.

BUCKINGHAMSHIRE RECORD OFFICE *Records of the Archdeaconry of Buckingham.* Occasional publications **2**. Aylesbury: the Office, 1961. Includes listing of bishops' transcripts, summary list of wills, etc. (names not given), act books, glebe terriers, marriage papers, etc.

CHARLTON, SARAH. 'Diocesan records', *O.* **10**(4), 1986, 123-6. Relating to Buckinghamshire.

The Archdeaconry became a part of the Diocese of Oxford at the Reformation. Two articles provide brief general introductions to diocesan records of genealogical interest—although both are now rather out of date:

'Genealogical sources within the Diocese of Oxford', *Oxfordshire Family Historian* **1**(1), 1977, 4-6. Brief discussion of parish registers, probate records, marriage bonds, etc.

PHILIP, I.G. 'Diocesan records in the Bodleian Library', *Genealogists' magazine* **8**(1), 1938, 7-9. The Diocesan records are now in the Oxfordshire Record Office.

Prior to the Reformation, the Archdeaconry was a part of the Diocese of Lincoln. Its records are described in:

MAJOR, KATHLEEN. *A handlist of the records of the Bishop of Lincoln, and of the Archdeacons of Lincoln and Stow.* O.U.P., 1953.

In addition to the local repositories, a major Buckinghamshire archival collection is to be found as far afield as California. A full description is given in:

'Stowe collection', in *Guide to British historical manuscripts in the Huntington Library.* San Marino, California: Huntington Library, 1982, 145-274. Guide to the papers of the Grenville, Temple, Nugent and Brydges family, medieval-19th c., which relate to properties in Buckinghamshire, and many other counties.

See also:

JENKINS, JOHN GILBERT. *A handlist of the Stowe Collection in the Huntington Library, California.* B.R.S. Lists and indexes **1**, 1956.

JENKINS, J.G. *The Stowe collection of manuscripts in the Huntington Library, California.* [High Wycombe: Buckinghamshire Record Society], 1954. Lecture.

3. JOURNALS AND NEWSPAPERS

Every genealogist with Buckinghamshire interests should join one of the local family history societies. Both of them publish journals which contain much information of value, and enable you to make contact with others researching the same lines. See:

Origins: magazine of the Buckinghamshire Family History Society. The Society, 1977- . Alternative title on early issues: *Buckinghamshire genealogy.* Sub-title varies; originally the *bulletin.*

Bucks ancestor: magazine of the Buckinghamshire Genealogical Society. 1992-

For the Buckinghamshire Family History Society in general, see:

ALLABY, SUE, & ALLABY, MARK. 'Buckinghamshire Family History Society', *Family tree magazine* **8**(10), 1992, 23.

The major historical journal for the county, which includes many articles of genealogical interest, is:

Records of Buckinghamshire, or, papers and notes on the history, antiquities and architecture of the county, together with the transactions of the Architectural and Archaeological Society for the County of Buckingham. Aylesbury: the Society, 1858- . This is indexed in: BRADBROOK, W., & ELAND, G. *Index to Records of Bucks., vols. I to X.* [ ]: Architectural & Archaeological Society for the County of Buckingham, 1928, and in: HEAD, LORNA M. *Records of Buckinghamshire: index to volumes XI to XX (1919-1978).* 1992.

See also:

The Berks, Bucks & Oxon archaeological journal. 34 vols. Oxford: Berkshire Archaeological Society, 1889-1930. Continued by *The Berkshire Archaeological Journal.* This is indexed in:

BUNCE, F.M. *Index of the Berks, Bucks & Oxon Archaeological Journal and of the Quarterly Journal of the Berks Archaeological Society, Volumes 1-3, 1890-5, Berks Archaeological Journal, Volumes 1-25, 1895-1919, Berks, Bucks and Oxon Archaeological Journal.* Oxford: Basil Blackwell for the Berkshire Archaeological Society, [1924]. Reprinted from: *B.B.O.A.J.* **28**(2), 1924, 1-24.

Home Counties Magazine, devoted to the topography of London, Middlesex, Essex, Herts, Bucks, Berks, Surrey and Kent. 14 vols. F.E. Robinson & Co., 1899-1912. Indexed in *Home Counties Magazine: General Index to volumes I-X.* G. Bell & Sons, [1911?].

The publications of record societies often include works vital to the genealogist. Many are listed in appropriate places below. For Buckinghamshire, consult:

Buckinghamshire Archaeological Society Records Branch publications 1937-45. Continued by:

Buckinghamshire Record Society 1947-

Useful local journals include:

Chess Valley Archaeological and Historical Society newletter 1973-80. Continued by:

Chess Valley: journal of the Chess Valley Archaeological & Historical Society 1981- . Includes news, book reviews and a few brief articles.

Milton Keynes journal of archaeology and history. Wolverton: Wolverton and District Archaeological Society, 1972-

For newspapers, consult:

Handlist of local newspapers in Buckinghamshire County Library. Aylesbury: the Library, 1990.

McLAUGHLIN, EVE. 'News to you', *O.* **10**(2), 1986, 63. Lists 19th c. newspapers in Buckinghamshire libraries.

4. PEDIGREES, HERALDRY AND BIOGRAPHICAL DICTIONARIES, *etc.*

In the sixteenth and seventeenth centuries, the Heralds undertook 'visitations' of the counties in order to determine the right of gentry to bear heraldic arms. One consequence of this activity was the compilation of pedigrees for most of the gentry. The visitation returns continue to be important sources of genealogical information. See:

METCALFE, WALTER C., ed. *The Visitation of Buckinghamshire in 1566, by William Harvey, Clarenceulx Rex Armorum, (Harleian ms. 5867).* Exeter: William Pollard, 1883. Reprinted from *Genealogist* 7, 1883, 116-22, 172-89 & 244-57.

RYLANDS, W. HARRY, ed. *The Visitation of the County of Buckingham made in 1634 by John Philipott, esq., Somerset Herald, and William Ryley, Bluemantel pursuivant, marshals and deputies to Sir Richard St.George, knight, Clarenceaux, and Sir John Borough, knight, Garter, who visited as Norroy by mutual agreement; including the church notes then taken, together with pedigrees from the visitation made in 1566 by William Harvey, esq., Clarenceux, and some pedigrees from other sources.* Publication of the Harleian Society 58, 1909.

The heralds also had responsibility for granting arms, and for conducting funerals of the armigerous classes. A few grants of arms, funeral certificates, etc., relating to specific Buckinghamshire families are printed, and are listed here.

Chase
'Funeral certificate of Matthew Chase of Chesham, Co.Bucks, gent., 1638', *M.G.H.* 2, 1877, 481.

Cooke
'Confirmation of arms and grant of crest to Sir Richard Cooke, knight, 1612', *M.G.H.* 5th series 7, 1929-31, 309.

Garrard
GOWER, GRANVILLE LEVESON. 'Funeral certificate: Sir William Garrard, 1607', *M.G.H.* 2nd series 1, 1886, 52. Of Dorney.

Gyll
'Armorial book-plates: Gordon Willoughby James Gyll', *M.G.H.* 2, 1876, 130.

Hatcliffe
'Funeral certificate: William Hatcliffe, 1620', *M.G.H.* N.S. 4, 1884, 218.

Mundy
CLARK-MAXWELL, W.G. 'A grant of arms of the year 1510', *Archaeologia* 83, 1933, 167-70. To John Mundy, of High Wycombe.

Penyston
'Confirmation of arms to Thomas Penyston of Hawruge, Bucks', *Genealogist* 1, 1877, 1-5. See also 2, 1878, 26-7.

Power
RYLANDS, J. PAUL. 'Confirmation of arms to John Power, of the County of Buckingham, gentleman, 1478', *M.G.H.* 4th series 3, 1910, 273.

An important collection of pedigrees is also to be found in:

BERRY, WILLIAM. *County genealogies: Pedigrees of Buckinghamshire families.* Sherwood Gilbert and Piper, 1837.

A number of biographical dictionaries—some giving pedigrees as well—are available:

GRANT, JOHN. *Buckinghamshire: a short history with genealogies and current biographies.* London & Provincial Publishing, 1912.

GIBBS, ROBERT. *Worthies of Buckinghamshire, and men of note of that County.* Aylesbury: Bucks Advertiser & Aylesbury News, 1888.

COPPOCK, J.C. *Some local men of mark in South Bucks: a series of biographical sketches reprinted from the South Bucks Standard.* High Wycombe: South Bucks Standard, 1892.

SPALDING, RUTH. *Contemporaries of Bulstrode Whitelocke, 1605-75: biographies illustrated by letters and other documents.* Oxford University Press, 1989. Biographical dictionary of persons mentioned in his letters, including many from Buckinghamshire.

STERN, JULIUS LONG. 'Worthies of Buckinghamshire as Members of Parliament and as Justices of the Peace, 1678-1689', *R.o.B.* 17(1), 1961, 3-19. Includes lists.

PRESS, C.A. MANNING. *Buckinghamshire leaders, social and political.* Gaskill Jones & Co., 1905. Contemporary.

PIKE, W.T. *Berks, Bucks & Beds: in the twentieth century: contemporary biographies.* Brighton: W.T. Pike & Co., 1907.

PIKE, W.T., ed. *Bucks, Beds and Hertfordshire: contemporary biographies.* Brighton: W.T. Pike, 1908. Cover title.

VERNEY, MARGARET M. *Bucks biographies.* Oxford: Clarendon Press, 1912.

Who's who in Buckinghamshire. Who's Who in the Counties series, 1936.

Finally, no Buckinghamshire genealogist should fail to consult:

BUCKINGHAMSHIRE FAMILY HISTORY SOCIETY *Directory of members interests.* [2nd ed]. [ ]: B.F.H.S., 1993. The first edition was published in 1979; it may still be worth consulting this and its four supplements. The new directory will be updated quarterly in *Origins*.

5. OCCUPATIONAL SOURCES

Many works offer biographical information on men (rarely women!) of particular occupations. These are listed here. For clergymen, see section 12, teachers and students, section 15, government officials, section 14. See also *Occupational Sources for Genealogists*.

Chairmakers

McLAUGHLIN, EVE. 'The Wycombe chairmakers, 1851', *O.* **8**(1), 1984, 22-5. List from the census.

Clockmakers

LEGG, EDWARD. *The clock and watchmakers of Buckinghamshire.* Occasional paper **3**. Milton Keynes: Bradwell Abbey Field Centre, 1976. List with biographical notes. See also *O.* **11**(4), 1987, 124-8.

Convicts

COLDHAM, PETER WILSON. *Bonded passengers for America, vol.7: Norfolk Circuit, comprising the counties of Bedfordshire, Buckinghamshire, Cambridgeshire, Huntingdonshire, Norfolk and Suffolk.* Baltimore: Genealogical Publishing, 1983. Lists convicts transported.

McLAUGHLIN, EVE, ed. *Bucks convicts: list of men transported to Australia, 1789-1860.* 2nd ed. Haddenham: Buckinghamshire Publications, 1993.

LAMBERT, HOWARD. 'Sent to the hulks', *O.* **11**(4), 1987, 140-41. Brief list of prisoners sent to the Portsmouth hulks in 1830 for transportation.

McL[AUGHLIN], E. 'Criminal connections', *O.* **6**(4), 1982, 94-5. Brief list of 18th c. convicts.

East India Men

'Buckinghamshire recruits to the East India Company's army, 1778-1786', *O.* **8**(4), 1985, 109-13. List, giving occupation, age, height, date and ship.

DAVIES, LESLEY WYNNE. 'More wretched objects', *O.* **9**(1), 1985, 32-4. Ditto for 1786-8.

Farmers

McLAUGHLIN, EVE. 'A murrain on Marsh Gibbon', *O.* **5**(3), 1981, 22. List of farmers claiming compensation for the cattle plague of 1866, from Quarter Sessions records.

McLAUGHLIN, EVE. 'The Buckingham farmers', *O.* **6**(4), 1982, 87. List of opponents of the Anti-Corn Law League, 1844.

Freemasons

ELLISTON, R.J. *A short history of Buckingham Lodge no.591 (formerly no.861) from its consecration in 1852 to its jubilee in 1902.* [ ]: privately published, 1917. Includes chronological list of members.

Hospital Subscribers

McLAUGHLIN, EVE. 'The Royal Bucks Hospital', *Bucks ancestor* **1**(1), 1992, 15-17. Includes names of original subscribers of this Aylesbury hospital, 1830-33.

Innkeepers

'Did Grandpa keep a pub?', *O.* **14**(4), 1990, 125-32. Sources for innkeepers.

Millers

McLAUGHLIN, EVE. 'The mills of Bucks', *O.* **13**(4), 1989, 133-4. List of millers, 1798.

Needlemakers

SHRIMPTON, BERT. 'Migration 1844: how a party of Long Crendon needlemakers migrated to Worcestershire', *O.* **9**(2), 1985, 48-51.

Pipemakers

AYTO, ERIC G. 'Notes on clay tobacco pipes found in the district of Eton and Slough', *News Bulletin of the Middle Thames Archaeological and Historical Society* **2**(16), 1971, 104-9. Includes some names.

AYTO, ERIC G. 'Pipe makers of Eton, *News Bulletin of the Middle Thames Archaeological and Historical Society* **3**(17), 1972, 122-4. Includes list.

Policemen

'Buckinghamshire Constabulary roll of honour 1914-18 and 1939-45', *O.* **17**(1), 1993, 44. 36 names.

Postmasters

KEARVALL, GORDON. 'Post Office and postmasters', *News Bulletin of the Middle Thames Archaeological and Historical Society* **20**, 1975, 20. Includes list of Slough postmasters, 1841-1971.

Rioters

CHAMBERS, JILL. *Buckinghamshire machine breakers: the story of the 1830 riots.* Letchworth: the author, 1991. Includes a biographical dictionary of rioters, with lists of special constables, etc.

DELL, ALAN, et al. 'The Captain Swing riots in Bucks', *O.* **6**(4), 1992, 96-103. Includes list of those convicted of machine breaking in the 1831 riots.

Sailors

ASHFORD, PAM. 'Bucks men at Trafalgar', *O.* **16**(4), 1992, 160. Gives age, rank, and place of birth of those who served.

Servants

DAVIES, LESLEY WYNNE. 'Richard Hampden's servants in 1660', *O.* **9**(3), 1985, 109-12. Biographical notes on servants.

HORN, PAMELA. 'Upstairs, downstairs', *O.* **13**(2), 1989, 53-61. Servants.

Soldiers, *etc.*

Many Buckinghamshire men have served in the army or militia, and much information on them is available in the various regimental histories etc. which have been compiled—especially for the first world war. These cannot all be listed here. The works listed below include only those publications which have lists of officers and/or men, and which are therefore of direct genealogical value. The list is in rough chronological order. For works on musters and the early militia, see section 10. For war graves, see section 9A.

NEWBOLT, SIR HENRY JOHN. *The story of the Oxfordshire and Buckinghamshire Light Infantry (the old 43rd and 52nd Regiments).* George Newnes, 1915. Includes lists of officers and men, 1914-15, although the volume commences in 1741.

SWANN, JOHN CHRISTOPHER. *The citizen soldiers of Buckinghamshire, 1795-1926.* Buckinghamshire Territorial Army Association, 1930.

KILLON, M.R. 'The Royal Bucks Militia in Maidstone', *O.* **5**(1), 1981, 21. Extracts from registers of Maidstone, Kent, 1804-5.

NEVILLE, J.E.H. *History of the 43rd and 52nd (Oxfordshire and Buckinghamshire) Light Infantry in the Great War, 1914-1919.* Aldershot: Gale & Polden, 1938. Intended as a multi-volume work, but only vol.1 was published. Includes various lists of officers and men.

PICKFORD, P. *War record of the 1/4th Battalion Oxfordshire & Buckinghamshire Light Infantry.* [Banbury]: Banbury Guardian, 1919. Extensive lists.

STEWART-LIBERTY, IVOR. *A record of the 2nd Bucks Battalion T.F. 1914-1918.* Chesham: Carlton Press, 1918. Various lists of officers and men.

Soldiers, *etc. continued*

SWANN, JOHN CHRISTOPHER. *The 2nd Bucks Battalion, Oxfordshire and Buckinghamshire Light Infantry, 1914-1918.* [ ]: Buckinghamshire Territorial Force Association, [1929]. Includes various lists of officers and men.

WHEELER, C. *Memorial record of the Seventh (Service) Battalion, the Oxfordshire and Buckinghamshire Light Infantry.* Oxford: Basil Blackwell, 1921. Includes roll of honour and other lists, 1914-19.

WRIGHT, P.L. *The First Buckinghamshire Battalion, 1914-1919.* Hazell Watson & Viney, 1920. Includes various lists of officers and men.

The Oxfordshire and Buckinghamshire Light Infantry. [ ]: [ ], [1919?]. Roll of honour, 1914-19.

[SUTTON, I.] *This roll of honour is dedicated to the memory of 5878 officers, warrant officers, non-commissioned officers and men of the Oxfordshire and Buckinghamshire Light Infantry who gave their lives in the Great War 1914 to 1919.* Oxford: O.U.P., [1919?].

Soldiers died in the Great War, 1914-1918, part 47: the Oxfordshire and Buckinghamshire Light Infantry. H.M.S.O., 1921. Reprinted Polstead: J.B. Hayward, 1989.

Roll of honour (Farnham Royal and district 1914-1919). Farnham Common: Reuben Lund, [1920?].

'Almost all they had they gave', *O.* **13**(1), 1989, 29. Medmenham soldiers, 1914-18, commemorated in the church.

The Oxfordshire and Buckinghamshire Light Infantry. [ ]: [ ], c.1945. Roll of honour, 1939-45.

Swan Owners

TICEHURST, N.F. 'The swan-marks of Oxfordshire and Buckinghamshire', *Oxford Archaeological Society transactions and reports* **82**, 1936, 97-130. Lists 175 16th c. swan owners.

Tradesmen

In an age when coins were in short supply, tradesmen frequently issued their own tokens. There are a number of studies of these tokens for Buckinghamshire, providing information which may be of genealogical value.

MANTON, JAS. O., & HOLLIS, EDWIN. *Buckinghamshire trade tokens issued in the seventeenth century.* Aylesbury: Buckinghamshire Archaeological Society, 1933. Reprinted from the *British Numismatic Journal.*

BERRY, G., & MORLEY, P. 'A revised survey of the seventeenth-century tokens of Buckinghamshire', *British Numismatic Journal* **43**, 1973, 96-125. Revision of Manton.

BERRY, GEORGE. 'Notes on the seventeenth-century token issuers of Chesham', *R.o.B.* **18**(5), 1970, 422-6. Includes biographical notes.

BERRY, GEORGE. 'New light on the seventeenth century token issuers of Chepping Wycombe', *R.o.B.* **18**(2), 1967, 150-63. Includes biographical notices.

6. FAMILY HISTORIES, *etc.*

Adeane

See Dene

Allnutt

NOBLE, ARTHUR H. *The families of Allnutt and Allnatt*. Aylesbury: Dolphin, 1912. Of Oxfordshire, Buckinghamshire, Berkshire, etc., 16-20th c. Includes pedigrees and wills.

Astor

KAVALER, LUCY. *The Astors: a family chronicle*. Harrap, 1966.

Baldwin

CHESTER, JOSEPH LEMUEL. *Investigations concerning the family of Baldwin of Aston Clinton, Bucks*. Boston: [ ], 1884. Reprinted from the *Historical and Genealogical Register*. 17th c.

Bard

S., G.S. 'Pedigree of Bard, of Lincolnshire, Middlesex and Bucks., and Viscount Bellamont of the Kingdom of Ireland', *Collectanea topographica et genealogica* **4**, 1837, 59-61. 16-18th c.

Barker

'Pedigree of Barker of Great Horwood, Co.Bucks, and of Newbury, Co.Berks', *M.G.H.* 3rd series **3**, 1900, 142-7. 17-18th c.

Barnard

BLOOM, J. HARVEY. 'Pedigree of Barnard', *M.G.H.* 5th series **7**, 1929-31, 304-6. Of Bedfordshire, Buckinghamshire, etc., 17th c. Includes wills, deeds, etc.

Bellamont

See Bard

Bernard

HIGGINS, MRS NAPIER. *The Bernards of Abington and Nether Winchendon: a family history.* 4 vols. Longmans Green & Co., 1903-4. Medieval-19th c.

Blackwell

COLEMAN, MR. 'Blackwell', *M.G.H.* N.S. **1**, 1874, 177-8. Of Buckinghamshire and Hertfordshire; notes from early 17th c. deeds.

Blundell

BLUNDELL, JOS. HIGHT. 'Blundell of Great Linford and Cardington, with Irish connections', *M.G.H.* 5th series **6**, 1926-8, 264-8. 16-19th c. Cardington, Bedfordshire.

Boddington

BODDINGTON, REGINALD STEWART. 'Boddington or Bodington genealogy', *M.G.H.* N.S. **2**, 1877, 163-4. Includes pedigree and notes on monumental inscriptions at Brayfield, 15-17th c.

Boteler

See Turville

Boughton

McLAUGHLIN, TERENCE. 'Worthies of Bucks, 4: Rutland Boughton, 1878-1960', *O.* **2**(2), 1978, 19-21. Includes pedigree, 18-20th c.

Bradbrooke

BRADBROOK, WILLIAM. *The Bradbrooke family register.* Privately printed, 1935. Medieval-20th c., of Norfolk, Buckinghamshire, Bethnal Green, Middlesex, Inkberrow, Worcestershire, etc.

Briden

BRIDEN, EDWARD JOHN. *The Bridens of Markyate.* Chalfont St.Peter: Briden, 1981.

Brise

See Way

Brocas

BURROWS, MONTAGU. *The family of Brocas of Beaurepaire and Roche Court ...* Longmans Green & Co., 1886. Includes folded pedigree, medieval-19th c.

Brooke

See Wittewronge

Brudenell

WAKE, JOAN. *The Brudenells of Deene.* 2nd ed. Cassell, 1954. Deene, Northants. The family had early Buckinghamshire connections. Includes folded pedigree, 15-20th c.

Burrows

BURROWS, MONTAGU. *History of the family of Burrows of Sydenham and Long Crendon.* Oxford: E. Pickard Hall, 1877. Includes folded pedigree, 18-19th c.

Cantilupe

See Ingleton

Capper

See Wittewronge

Chester

WATERS, ROBERT EDMOND CHESTER. *Genealogical memoirs of the extinct family of Chester, of Chicheley, their ancestors and descendants.* 2 vols. Robson & Sons, 1878. Includes many pedigrees of related families.

Chesterfield

See Wharton

Chetwood

TUCKER, STEPHEN. *Pedigree of the family Chetwode of Chetwode, Co.Bucks., of Oakley, Co.Stafford, Worleston, Co.Chester, and of Warkworth, Co.Northampton, with their charters and other evidences, to which is added report and papers connected with their claim to the Barony of De Wahull, and an account of the Chetwode Rhyme Toll.* Mitchell & Hughes, 1884. Includes pedigrees, medieval-18th c., with deeds, monumental inscriptions, parish register extracts, etc.

'The true pedegree & descent of ye auntient & right worshipfull familie of Chetwood of Chetwood, & Warleston, Hoclyue & Warkeworth as they are descended from the most auncient barons of Wahull alias Woodhull in the County of Bedford, & Leon in ye countie of Northampton ...', *M.G.H.* 2nd series **1**, 1886, 69-88. Chetwood, Buckinghamshire, Hockliffe, Bedfordshire, Warkworth, Northamptonshire and Worleston, Cheshire. 11-18th c., includes deed abstracts.

Cheney

See De la Vache

Clinkard

WEBSTER, ANGELA. 'The Clinkards of Ibstone', *O.* **5**(4), 1981, 24-5. 18-19th c.

Clinton

See Fynes-Clinton

Cobham

'Pedigree of John Lord Cobham', *R.o.B.* **1**, 1858, 218. 13-14th c.

Cooke

See Way

Coventry

See Darby-Coventry

Cowper

Cowper memorials: records of the Rev. John Cowper, M.A., and other members of the family of William Cowper, the poet. Olney: Oliver Ratcliffe, 1904.

Cox

ADKINS, BARBARA. 'The Cox family of Waddesdon', *O.* **3**(1), 1979, 10-11. 18-19th c.

See also Honour

Croke

CROKE, SIR ALEXANDER. *The genealogical history of the Croke family, originally named Le Blount.* 2 vols. J. Murray, 1823.

Cullum

See Wittewronge

Danvers

MACNAMARA, F.N. *Memorials of the Danvers family (of Dauntsey and Culworth), their ancestors and descendants from the Conquest till the termination of the eighteenth century, with some account of the alliances of the family, and of the places where they were seated.* Hardy & Page, 1895. Dauntsey, Wiltshire; Culworth, Northamptonshire. Includes medieval pedigree of Danvers of Buckinghamshire, Berkshire and Oxfordshire, etc.

Darby-Coventry

FELL, S.G. *The family of Darby-Coventry of Greenlands, Henley on Thames.* Leadenhall Press, 1892. 15-19th c.

Dashwood

DASHWOOD, SIR FRANCIS. *The Dashwoods of West Wycombe.* Aurum, 1987.

Dayrell

DAYRELL, ELEANORA. *The history of the Dayrells of Lillingstone Dayrell from William the Conqueror to Victoria, with mention of the families of Grenville, Seymour, Neville, Hampden, Carew, Purefoy, Trelawney, and the royal family of England, into which they have intermarried.* Jersey: Le Lievre Bros., 1885.

Deane

See Dene

De Bolebec

MARSH, J. 'On the noble family De Bolebec', *R.o.B.* **1**, 1858, 246-54. Medieval.

De la Vache

H., W. 'De La Vache, Restwold and Cheyney', *M.G.H.* **2**, 1876, 134-5. Of Buckinghamshire, Yorkshire, etc., pedigree, 14-18th c.

Delafield

DELAFIELD, JOHN ROSS. *Delafield: the family history*. 2 vols. New York: privately printed, 1945. Of Ireland, Buckinghamshire, the United States, etc., medieval-20th c. Includes many extracts from original sources.

Dell

DELL, ALAN. 'John Dell of Aylesbury: brewer and politician', *O.* **3**(3), 1979, 23-6. Includes Dell pedigree, 18-20th c.

Dene

DEANE, MARY. *The book of Dene, Deane, Adeane: a genealogical history*. Elliot Stock, 1899. Of Buckinghamshire and various other counties, medieval-19th c.

Denham

See Dinham

Deverell

DEVERILL, PENELOPE. 'The medieval Deverells of Wilts and Bucks', *O.* **15**(4), 1991, 95-6.

Dinham

GREEN, EVERARD. 'Pedigree of the family of Dinham (Dynham, Denham) of Stamford and Spalding, Co.Lincoln, descended from the family of Dinham of Boarstall, Co. Buckingham', *M.G.H.* 4th series **2**, 1908, 17-20. 16-19th c.

Dormer

MACLAGAN, MICHAEL. 'The family of Dormer in Oxfordshire and Buckinghamshire', *Oxoniensia* **11**, 1946-7, 90-101. Includes pedigree, 16-18th c.

TRAPPES-LOMAX, T.B. 'Some homes of the Dormer family', *Recusant history* **8**, 1965-6, 178-87. 15-20th c.

See also Way

Duket

DICKETT, SIR G.F. *Duchetiana, or, historical and genealogical memoirs of the family of Duket, from the Conquest to the present time, in the counties of Lincoln, Westmoreland, Wilts, Cambridge, and Buckingham, comprising the houses of Grayrigg, Hartham, Steeple-Morden, Aylesbury and Wycombe, with the several ancient families from whom they descend*. J. Russell Smith, 1869. Includes pedigrees and many extracts from the public records, monumental inscriptions, etc.

Duncombe

DUNCOMBE, R.F. 'Duncombe of Buckinghamshire', *O.* **1**(4), 1977, 27-9. Includes pedigree, 16-17th c.

Dynham

See Dinham

Egerton

HARINGTON, D.W. 'The Egerton family of Adstock in the County of Buckingham', *Family history* **9**, 1975, 93-128.

Etheredge

Genealogical memoranda relating to the family of Etheredge, compiled from the Etheredge bible in the possession of Percy C.S. Bruere, esq. Mitchell & Hughes, 1873. Reprinted from *M.G.H.* 17-18th c.

Eure

See Fynes-Clinton

Eustace

EUSTACE, DONALD W. *The Eustaces of the Chiltern Hundreds*. 2 vols. The author, 1974-9. Oxfordshire, Berkshire, Buckinghamshire, etc., medieval-20th c.

Evelyn

'Evelyn of Huntercombe, Co.Bucks', *M.G.H.* 2nd series **4**, 1892, 328. Pedigree, 17th c.

Ferrers

FERRERS, CECIL S.F. 'William Ferrers of Taplow, Bucks', *Ancestor* **8**, 1904, 226-7. 15th c.

Ffarington

See Way

Finch

FINCH, JOYCE & JOHN. *Jane Finch and her family*. Worthing: Denham House, 1974. Of Buckinghamshire and Surrey; includes folded pedigree, 18-20th c.

Fleetwood

'Pedigree of the Fleetwoods of The Vache, in Chalfont St.Giles', *R.o.B.* **6**, 1887, 106-7. 15-17th c.

Fowler

CARTER, WILLIAM F. 'The Fowlers of Hambleton', *Genealogist* **7**, 1883, 4-10. Hambleton, Rutland; also of Oxfordshire, Bedfordshire and Buckinghamshire. Includes wills, 16-17th c.

Freeman

TYACK, GEOFFREY. 'The Freemans and their buildings', *R.o.B.* **24**, 1982, 130-43. 17-19th c.

Fynes-Clinton

CRAIK, ANNA. *Annals of our ancestors: some records and recollections of the families of Fynes-Clinton and Matthews (Eure of Witton).* Edinburgh: R.M. Clark, 1924. Includes many pedigrees, some folded. Witton is in Co.Durham.

Gardyner

'Pedigree of the Gardyners of The Grove, or Grove Place, Chalfont St.Giles', *R.o.B.* **6**, 1887, 108. 16-17th c.

Gery

See Wittewronge

Gibbs

REYNOLDS, C.F. *The Gibbs family of Aylesbury: an extract from the CODIL family history data base.* Uxbridge: the author, 1979. 18-19th c.

REYNOLDS, CHRIS. 'The Gibbs of Aylesbury', *O.* **3**(1), 1979, 12-13. 18-19th c.

Giffard

PARKER, JOHN. 'The Giffards', *R.o.B.* **7**, 1897, 475-510 & **8**, 1903, 289-308. Medieval.

Goodall

DELL, ALAN. 'Worthies of Bucks, 5: the Goodalls', *O.* **2**(3), 1978, 15-16 & **2**(4), 1978, 21-4. 18-19th c. Includes pedigree.

Grenville

SMITH, WILLIAM JAMES, ed. *The Grenville papers, being the correspondence of Richard Grenville, Earl Temple K.G., and the Right Hon. George Grenville, their friends and contemporaries.* 4 vols. John Murray, 1852-3.

TOMLINSON, JOHN, ed. *Additional Grenville papers, 1763-1765.* Manchester: M.U.P., 1962.

Gurney

WOODMAN, A. VERE. 'A fifteenth-century pedigree', *R.o.B.* **16**(1), 1953-4, 43-7. Gurney family.

'The Gurney papers', *O.* **5**(2), 48-9. Medieval-19th c.

Hampden

McLAUGHLIN, E. 'Hampden House and its owners', *O.* **13**(3), 1989, 88-9. Includes pedigree of Hampden, 16-18th c.

Harding

FORD, J.C. 'Extract from a family register', *M.G.H.* N.S. **1**, 1874, 357. Harding family of Amersham, 16th c.

Hawtrey

HAWTREY, FLORENCE MOLESWORTH. *The history of the Hawtrey family.* 2 vols. George Allen, 1903. Includes folded pedigree, medieval-19th c.

Hill

See Way

Honour

ADKINS, BARBARA. 'The Honours of Stanbridge in the parish of Leighton Buzzard, Beds', *O.* **5**(3), 1981, 24. Pedigree, 16-19th c., showing connection with Cox of Waddesdon.

Ingleton

LAMBARDE, FANE. 'Robert Ingelton, jentilman', *M.G.H.* 5th series **9**, 1935-7, 98-100. Includes pedigrees of Ingleton and Cantilupe, 15th c.

Ingoldsby

'Pedigree of Ingoldsby', *Genealogist* N.S. **3**, 1886, 136-9. 16-18th c.

Ivatts

IVATTS, EDMUND B. *Notes on the family names of Ivatt and Ivatts.* Birmingham: E.B. Ivatts, 1906. Mainly 17-18th c.

Jenkins

JENKINS, THOMAS BLYFORD. *A brief review of the descendants of William Jenkins of Aylesbury who died 1798, with notes, biographies and genealogical tables to 1927.* Bexleyheath: Thos. William Jenkins, 1928. Includes pedigrees, 18-20th c.

Kenrick

See Way

King

'Notices of the King family', *R.o.B.* **4**, 1870, 84-9. 16-17th c.

Knapp

Pedigree of Mathew Grenville Samwell Knapp of Little Linford, Bucks and of Arthur John Knapp of Llanfoist House, Clifton Down, Bristol. Mitchell & Hughes, 1879. Reprinted from *M.G.H.* N.S. **3**, 1880, 261-4. 16-19th c.

Lane

'Pedigree of Lane from visitation of Bucks, 1634, in College of Arms', *M.G.H.* N.S. **1**, 1874, 186.

Lawes

See Wittewronge

Langley

'Langley bookplates', *M.G.H.* 2nd series **4**, 1892, 184-5. Langley family of Great Marlow; includes pedigree, 16-19th c.

Le Blount

See Croke

Lee

BUCKINGHAMSHIRE RECORD OFFICE *The Lees of Hartwell: catalogue of an exhibition of documents, portraits, etc., depicting the life of a county family held at the County Museum, Aylesbury, 23 June—14 July 1962.* [Aylesbury]: the Office, 1962. Mainly 17-18th c.

L[EE], F.G. 'The Lees of Quarrendon', *Herald & genealogist* **3**, 1886, 113-22, 289-95 & 481-7. 15-19th c.

LEE, FREDERICK GEORGE. 'The Lees of Quarrendon', *R.o.B.* **3**, 1870, 203-14 & 214-49. Medieval-17th c.

LEE, FREDERICK GEORGE. 'Pedigree of the family of Lee, Co's Chester, Bucks and Oxon', *M.G.H.* 2nd series **1**, 1886, 101-8, 127-32 & 147-8. 14-19th c.

LEE, RUPERT HENRY MELVILLE. *Related to Lee.* 3 pts. Oxford: the author, 1963-4. Of Buckinghamshire, Oxfordshire, Cheshire, etc., medieval-20th c.

Le Heup

See Wittewronge

Longueville

E., D.C. 'Longueville, of Overton Longueville, Co.Huntingdon, eventually of Wolverton, Co.Bucks', *Herald & genealogist* **6**, 1871, 49-53. Pedigree, 13-18th c.

'Longueville family: extracts from the Wolverton registers', *M.G.H.* **1**, 1868, 64-5. 16-17th c.

Lovegrove

BLOOM, J. HARVEY. 'Bible entries: Lovegrove', *M.G.H.* 5th series **6**, 1926-8, 434-7. Of Great Marlow, 18-19th c.

Lucy

FAIRFAX-LUCY, ALICE. *Charlcote and the Lucys: the chronicle of an English family.* O.U.P., 1958. 12-20th c.

Matthews

See Fynes-Clinton

Maunsell

COKAYNE, GEORGE EDWARD. 'Pedigree of Maunsell, formerly of Chicheley, Bucks., and subsequently, after 1622, of Thorpe manor, Co. Northampton, enlarged and continued from that entered in the visitation of Essex, A.D. 1634', *Genealogist* N.S. **19**, 1903, 12-18, 88-96, 153-8 & 235-41. Includes wills, monumental inscriptions and parish register extracts.

Montfort

PAYNE, E.J. 'The Montforts, the Wellesbournes, and the Hughendon effigies', *R.o.B.* **7**, 1897, 362-412. Medieval; includes pedigree of Montfort.

Newnham

See Way

Norman

See Way

North

'North', *M.G.H.* **2**, 1876, 94-5. Of Buckinghamshire and Oxfordshire, 18th c.

Packington

BARNARD, E.A.B. 'The Packingtons of Westwood', *Transactions of the Worcestershire Archaeological Society* **13**, 1936, 28-49. Westwood, Worcestershire; also of Buckinghamshire. 16-19th c.

Page

See Way

Palmer

ROCHE, T.W.E. 'The Palmers of Dorney', *Family history* **14/15**, 1972, 65-9.

Parker

LEARY, JOHN E. *The Quainton and American Parkers: the story of a lowly family.* Hornchurch: Leary, 1971. 17-20th c., includes pedigree.

Paxton

See Way

Payne

See Way

Penington

See Penn

Penn

HOGG, O.F.G. *Further light on the ancestry of William Penn.* Society of Genealogists, 1964. Penn of Buckinghamshire, Wiltshire, Hertfordshire, Shropshire, Gloucestershire and Wiltshire. Includes pedigrees, 12-18th c.

WEBB, MARIA. *The Penns and Peningtons of the seventeenth century in their domestic and religious life illustrated by original family letters, also incidental notices of their friend Thomas Ellwood with some of his unpublished verse.* F.B. Kitto, 1867.

Plaistead

PLAISTEAD, ARTHUR H. *The Plaistead family of North Wilts; with some account of the branches of Berks, Bucks, Somerset and Sussex.* Westminster Pub. Co., 1939.

Pontifex

PONTIFEX, E.C. *The family of Pontifex of West Wycombe, Co.Buckingham, 1500-1977.* Hassocks, Sussex: the author, 1977. Amendment 1, 1979. Includes folded pedigrees.

Purefoy

ELAND, G., ed. *Purefoy letters, 1735-1753.* 2 vols. Sidgwick & Jackson, 1931. Includes folded pedigree, 15-20th c.

MITCHELL, L.G., ed. *The Purefoy letters, 1735-1753.* Sidgwick & Jackson, 1973.

Puttenham

GRAHAM, NORMAN H. 'The Puttenham family of Puttenham and Long Marston, Co.Herts, and of Sherfield, Co.Hants., Puttnam (and Putnam) of Penn, etc., Co.Bucks, 1086-1956', *Notes & queries* **202**, 1957, 185-9 & 424-31; **204**, 1959, 50-56.

WOODMAN, A. VERE. 'Genealogical research in England: the origins of the Putenhams of Putnenham, Co.Herts., and Penn, Co.Bucks., England', *New England historical and genealogical register* **95**(2), 1941, 122-7. Medieval; includes pedigree.

Redrup

'The Redrup family in Bucks', *O.* **8**(1), 1984, 16-19. 16-18th c., includes pedigree.

Rose

GREEN, MILES, & CLARK, EVELYN. *The Rose family: Rayners and Tylers Green.* [Penn]: Penn & Tylers Green Jubilee Committee Local History Group, 1982. 19th c., includes list of tenants of the Rayners estate, 1920.

Rothschild

DAVIS, RICHARD. *The English Rothschilds.* Collins, 1983. 19-20th c.

DE ROTHSCHILD, MRS. JAMES. *The Rothschilds at Waddesdon Manor.* Collins, 1979. Includes pedigree, 18-20th c.

LOWE, MARGARET. 'What the butler saw', *O.* **10**(1), 1986, 15-19. Rothschild family; includes pedigree, 18-20th c.

MORTON, FREDERIC. *The Rothschilds: a family portrait.* Secker & Warburg, 1962. Includes folded pedigree, 18-20th c.

Rufford

GURNEY, FREDERICK G. 'Two XVth century neighbours in Edlesborough, and some coats of arms', *R.o.B.* **10**, 1916, 283-98. Rufford family.

Selby

Selbyana: an attempt to elucidate the origin and history of a once considerable family in the County of Buckingham, Selby of Wavendon. Carlisle: Francis Jollie, 1825. 17-19th c.

Sheffield

See Way

Skottowe

SKOTTOWE, PHILLIP F. *The leaf and the tree: the story of an English family.* Research Publishing, [1963]. Of Norfolk, Yorkshire, Buckinghamshire, etc., medieval-20th c.

Smyth

See Way

Stallworthy

STALLWORTHY, JON. *A familiar tree.* Chatto & Windus, 1978. Stallworthy family of Preston Bissett, 18-20th c., includes pedigree.

Stanley

See Way

Stonor

KINGSFORD, CHARLES LETHBRIDGE, ed. *The Stonor letters and papers, 1290-1483.* 2 vols. Camden 3rd series **29-30**. Royal Historical Society, 1919. See also **34**, 1912. Of Oxfordshire, Berkshire and Buckinghamshire; includes pedigree, 13-16th c.

Stratton

QUICK, BARBARA, & QUICK, KEVIN. 'At the heart of the community', *Bucks ancestor* **1**(1), 1992, 18-21. Stratton family. Mainly 18-19th c.

Stretley

MORIARTY, G. ANDREWS. 'The Stretley family of Bucks and Oxon', *R.o.B.* **13**, 1934-40, 379-97. Includes folded pedigree, medieval.

Taylor

See Way

Temple

GAY, EDWIN F. 'The rise of an English county family, Peter and John Temple, to 1603', *Huntington Library Quarterly* **1**(4), 1938, 367-90. Of Burton Dasset, Warwickshire, and Stowe, Buckinghamshire.

Temple *continued*

TEMPLE, JOHN ALEXANDER, & TEMPLE, HARALD MARKHAM. *The Temple memoirs: an account of this historic family and its demesnes with biographical sketches, anecdotes & legends from Saxon times to the present.* H.F. & G. Witherby, 1925. Includes folded pedigree.

Tothill

'The Shardeloes muniments', *R.o.B.* **14**, 1941-46, 164-73. Tothill family, 16-17th c.

Treacher

COLLINS, SIR WILLIAM J. 'Memorials of the Treacher family', *Transactions of the Baptist Historical Society* **2**(4), 1911, 5-23. 16-19th c., of Buckinghamshire and Hertfordshire.

Turville

MACMICHAEL, NICHOLAS H. 'A fourteenth century pedigree', *Genealogists' magazine* **12**(16), 1958, 535-9. Turville and Boteler families; includes pedigree.

Tyrrell

BROWN, O.F. *The Tyrrells of England.* Chichester: Phillimore, 1982.

Upton

See Way

Verey

VEREY, ALFRED. *The Verey family under southern skies: pedigree history England, Australia, New Zealand from 1522 to 1967.* Dandenong: Verey, 1967.

Verney

SANDFORD, MICHAEL. 'The Squire and his relations', *O.* **11**(3), 1987, 87-93. Verney family of Claydon; includes pedigree, 16-20th c.

BRUCE, JOHN, ed. *Letters and papers of the Verney family down to the end of the year 1639 ...* Camden Society **56**, 1853.

HORWOOD, ALFRED J. 'The manuscripts of Sir Harry Verney, Bart., at Claydon House, Co.Bucks', in HISTORICAL MANUSCRIPTS COMMISSION *Seventh report ...* C.2340. H.M.S.O., 1879, xiv, & 433-509. Mainly 17th c. letters.

SLATER, MIRIAM. *Family life in the seventeenth century: the Verneys of Claydon House.* Routledge & Kegan Paul, 1984. Includes pedigree.

SLATER, MIRIAM. 'The weightiest business: marriage in an upper-gentry family in seventeenth-century England', *Past and present* **72**, 1976, 25-54. See also **85**, 1979, 126-40.

BROAD, JOHN. 'Gentry finances and the Civil War: the case of the Buckinghamshire Verneys', *Economic history review* 2nd series **32**, 1979, 183-200. Includes pedigrees, 17-18th c.

BROAD, J.P.F. 'The Verneys and the sequestrators in the Civil Wars, 1642-56', *R.o.B.* **27**, 1985, 1-9.

PARTHENOPE, FRANCES LADY VERNEY. 'The house of Claydon and its inhabitants from 1480 to 1796', in her *Essays and tales.* Simpkins & Marshall, 1891, 15-24. This work also includes 'Three centuries of family portraits', 25-55.

VERNEY, FRANCES PARTHENOPE. *Memoirs of the Verney family during the Civil War ...* 2 vols. Longmans Green & Co., 1892. Reprinted Tabard Press, 1970. Includes folded pedigree, 13-17th c.

VERNEY, MARGARET M. *Memoirs of the Verney family during the Commonwealth, 1650 to 1660 ...* Longmans Green & Co., 1892. Reprinted Tabard Press, 1970.

VERNEY, MARGARET M. *Memoirs of the Verney family from the Restoration to the Revolution, 1660 to 1696.* Longmans Green & Co., 1892. Reprinted Tabard Press, 1970.

VERNEY, MARGARET MARIA. *Verney letters of the eighteenth century from the mss. at Claydon House.* 2 vols. Ernest Benn, 1930.

Watkins

RICHARDSON, W.M.H. 'Family register of the children of Sir David Watkins, Kt., temp. Car.I', *M.G.H.* N.S. **2**, 1877, 554-6. Of London and Chalfont St.Giles.

Way

STIRLING, A.M.W. *The Ways of yesterday being the chronicles of the Way family from 1307 to 1885.* Thornton Butterworth, 1930.

Way *continued*

WAY, HERBERT W.L. *History of the Way family: a record in chronological order of members of the Way family of Bridport, Co.Dorset, Denham Place, Co.Bucks, Spencer Grange and Spaynes Hall, Co.Essex, from the earliest records to the present time, with full or partial pedigrees of Page of Wricklemarsh, Newnham of Maresfield, Hill of Poundsford, Payne, Lord Sheffield, Lord Stanley of Alderley, Cooke, Taylor of Ogwell, Ruggles Brise of Spains Hall, Smyth of Ashton Court, Kenrick of Woore, Ffarington of Worden, Cottrell Dormer of Rousham, Upton of Ingmire, Paxton of Durham, Norman of Claverham, etc.* Harrison & Sons, 1914. Maresfield, Sussex; Alderley, Cheshire; Ogwell, Devon; Ashton Court, Somerset; Woore, Shropshire; Ingmire, Yorkshire; Durham, Co.Durham; Claverham, Somerset. Other places unidentified.

Weeden

BARTLETT, ELIZABETH. 'Genealogical research in England: Weeden', *New England Historical & Genealogical Register* **76**, 1922, 115-29. Includes wills, parish register abstracts, and pedigrees.

Wellesbourne

See Montfort

Wharton

PIGOTT, R.H. 'The Dukes of Wharton and Earl of Chesterfield', *R.o.B.* **7**, 1897, 247-61. 15-16th c.

White

WHITE, WILLIAM. *Some records prior to 1700 of White of Bedfordshire, Buckinghamshire, Hertfordshire, Huntingdonshire and a few of other shires, with incidental records of more than 80 other families.* Philadelphia: Allen Lane & Scott, 1945. Index to White records.

Wigg

ELVEY, GERALD, & ELVEY, ELIZABETH. *The Wiggs of Mentmore: the story of a Buckinghamshire family.* Buckingham: Barracuda, 1984. Includes pedigrees and extensive memorial inscription.

KIRBY, LEWIS, ed. *The Wigg family.* Phillimore, 1989. Reprints Elvey's *Wiggs of Mentmore* with Harold de Lorme's *The Wiggs of Beaufort.* Beaufort, Carolina, United States.

Wilde

BICKNELL, A. SIDNEY. *Five pedigrees: Bicknell of Taunton; Bicknell of Bridgwater; Bicknell of Farnham; Browne (Le Brune) of France and Spitalfields; Wilde of High Wycombe.* George Sherwood, 1912.

Wingate

WINGATE, CHARLES E.L. *History of the Wingate family in England and America, with genealogical tables.* Exeter, New Hampshire; James D.P. Wingate, 1886.

Wittewronge

CULLUM, GERY MILNER GIBSON. *Pedigree of Wittewronge of Ghent in Flanders, Stanton Barry (Bucks) and Rothamstead House (Herts), together with those of their descendants Lawes, Capper, Brooke, Gery, Le Heup and Cullum.* Mitchell Hughes & Clarke, 1905. Of London, Buckinghamshire and Herts, 15-19th c.

Wotton

ELAND, G., ed. *Thomas Wotton's letter-book, 1574-1586.* Oxford University Press, 1960. Includes pedigree of Wotton, 15-17th c.

7. PARISH REGISTERS AND OTHER RECORDS OF BIRTHS, MARRIAGES AND DEATHS

Parish registers are usually one of the first sources to be consulted by the genealogist. A full listing of manuscript parish registers is provided by:

WEBB, CLIFF. *National Index of Parish Registers, volume 9, part 3: Buckinghamshire.* Society of Genealogists, 1993.

See also:

McLAUGHLIN, EVE. *Bucks ancestry: parish registers, bishops transcripts, chapel registers, other parish records of genealogical value at the County Record Office.* 2nd ed. Haddenham: Buckinghamshire Publications, 1993.

A list of register transcripts held by the Buckinghamshire Archaeological Society is provided by:

E., E.M. 'Parish registers', *R.o.B.* **18**(2), 1967, 176-8.

Many Buckinghamshire registers are in print and are listed below. Be warned, however: just because a register has been printed does not necessarily mean that it is accurate. For a discussion of transcribers' errors, see:

'Can you trust Phillimore?', *O.* **12**(4), 1988, 138.

For a general discussion of mid-seventeenth century marriage records, see:

CLEAR, ARTHUR. 'Civil marriages during the Commonwealth', *R.o.B.* **7**, 1897, 531-7.

For Quaker marriages, see:

'Some early Quaker marriages in Bucks', *O.* **2**(4), 14. List of marriages in 1679.

'Quaker marriages in Bucks 1777-1794', *O.* **2**(1), 1978, 21-22. Excerpts from marriage registers.

Marriage indexes are essential tools for the genealogist. See:

'Marriage indexes', *Oxfordshire Family Historian* **1**(9), 1979, 247-50. Discusses a variety of indexes covering Oxfordshire, Berkshire, Northamptonshire, Warwickshire and Buckinghamshire.

Abstracts of a few marriage bonds are given in:

SHERWOOD, GEO. F. TUDOR. 'Bucks and Oxon marriage bonds', *B.B.O.A.J.* **2**, 1896, 52-8, 77-82 & 117-9.

Notes on 'stray' marriages, burials and deaths are regularly printed in *Origins*. See, for example:

'Married in Oxford', *O.* **8**(1), 1984, 27. List of Buckinghamshire marriages at Magdalen College, 1728-54, and St.Johns College, 1695-1752.

ADKINS, BARBARA, & MASON, EDNA. 'Bucks strays at Banbury', *O.* **5**(3), 1981, 10. 1710-1824.

Addington
USSHER, R., ed. *The register of the parish of Addington, Buckinghamshire.* B.P.R.S. **20**, 1916.

Amersham
GURNEY, THOS., ed. 'Marriages at Amersham, 1561 to 1812', in PHILLIMORE, W.P.W., & GURNEY, THOMAS, eds. *B.P.R.M.* **4**, *P.P.R.S.* **96**. Phillimore, 1908, 1-61.

Aston Abbots
BRADBROOK, WILLIAM, ed. *Buckinghamshire baptisms, marriages and burials: vol 1* (New series): Aston Abbots, 1559-1837; Edgcott, 1538-1837. B.P.R.S. **15**. Chas. A. Bernau, 1912.

BRADBROOK, WILLIAM. 'Aston Abbotts: parish register', *R.o.B.* **10**, 1916, 27-34. General discussion, with a few extracts.

Aston Clinton
RAGG, F.W., ed. 'Marriages at Aston Clinton, 1560 to 1812', in PHILLIMORE, W.P.W., & RAGG, F.W., eds. *B.P.R.M.* **2**, *P.P.R.S.* **40**. Phillimore, 1904, 115-40.

See also Saint Leonard

Beaconsfield
BEACONSFIELD AND DISTRICT HISTORICAL SOCIETY, ed. *The Beaconsfield parish register, 1600 to 1837.* Beaconsfield: the Society, 1973. Appendices include entries, 1540-1621, from the lost first volume of the register; also bishops' transcripts and list of dissenters' children.

GURNEY, THOMAS, ed. 'Marriages at Beaconsfield, 1631 to 1812', in PHILLIMORE, W.P.W., & GURNEY, THOMAS, eds. *B.P.R.M.* **5**, *P.P.R.S.* **123**. Phillimore, 1909, 1-30.

Bletchley
BRADBROOK, WILLIAM. 'Bletchley register', *R.o.B.* **8**, 1903, 234-48. General discussion, with list of family names.

Bow Brickhill
BLETCHLEY ARCHAEOLOGICAL AND HISTORICAL SOCIETY *All Saints, Bow Brickhill, Bucks., parish registers: baptisms, 1969-1991; marriages, 1837-1991; burials, 1885-1991.* Bletchley Archaeological & Historical Society, 1992.

Bradenham

GURNEY, THOMAS, ed. 'Marriages at Bradenham, 1627 to 1812', in PHILLIMORE, W.P.W., & GURNEY, THOMAS, eds. *B.P.R.M.* **6**, *P.P.R.S.* **134**. Phillimore, 1910, 125-32.

Broughton

BALE, R.F., ed. 'Marriages at Broughton, 1720 to 1837', in his *B.P.R.M.* **9**, *P.P.R.S.* **231**. Phillimore & Co., 1923, 139-45.

Burnham

GURNEY, THOMAS, ed. 'Marriages at Burnham, 1561 to 1812', in PHILLIMORE, W.P.W., & GURNEY. THOMAS, eds. *B.P.R.M.* **5**, *P.P.R.S.* **123**. Phillimore, 1909, 31-68.

N., J.G. 'Church notes of Burnham, Co.Buckingham, by the Rev. William Cole, F.S.A.', *Collectanea topographica et genealogica* **4**, 1837, 265-304. Includes parish register extracts, list of rectors and vicars, monumental inscriptions, etc.

Calverton

ELWES, DUDLEY GEORGE CARY. 'Notes from the registers of Calverton parish, Co.Bucks', *R.o.B.* **5**, 1878, 132-43. Includes extracts, with pedigree of Bennett, 16-18th c.

Chalfont St.Giles

GURNEY, THOS. 'Marriages at Chalfont St.Giles, 1584 to 1812', in PHILLIMORE, W.P.W., & GURNEY, THOMAS, eds. *B.P.R.M.* **4**, *P.P.R.S.* **96**. Phillimore, 1908, 79-103.

Chalfont St.Peter

GURNEY, THOS., ed. 'Marriages at Chalfont St.Peter, 1538 to 1812', in PHILLIMORE, W.P.W., & GURNEY, THOMAS, eds. *B.P.R.M.* **4**, *P.P.R.S.* **96**. Phillimore, 1908, 105-36.

GOSS, ROBERT. 'The Gold Hill Chapel, Chalfont St.Peter', *O.* **6**(2), 50-51. Extracts from the register, 1779-1836.

Chalvey

See Upton

Cheddington

'Marriages at Cheddington, 1552 to 1812', in PHILLIMORE, W.P.W., & RAGG, F.W., eds. *B.P.R.M.* **1**, *P.P.R.S.* **35**. Phillimore, 1902, 1-16.

Chenies

SHANN, REGINALD, ed. 'Marriages at Chenies, 1593 to 1836', in PHILLIMORE, W.P.W., & GURNEY, THOMAS, eds. *B.P.R.M.* **4**, *P.P.R.S.* **96**. Phillimore, 1908, 63-78.

Chesham

CHESS VALLEY ARCHAEOLOGICAL AND HISTORICAL SOCIETY *The people of Chesham: their births, marriages and deaths, 1637-1730.* Buckingham: Barracuda, 1984. Parish register; includes will of Susannah Carter, 1698.

GARRETT-PEGG, J.W., ed. *A transcript of the first volume, 1538-1636, of the parish register of Chesham, in the County of Buckingham, with introductory notes, appendices and index.* B.P.R.S. **4**. Elliot Stock, 1904. Includes list of vicars and churchwardens.

GURNEY, THOMAS, ed. 'Marriages at Chesham, 1637 to 1837', in PHILLIMORE, W.P.W., & GURNEY, THOMAS, eds. *B.P.R.M.* **8**, *P.P.R.S.* **177**. Phillimore, 1912, 33-154.

Chesham Bois

'Marriages in Chesham Bois, 1720-1743', *O.* **2**(4), 1978, 34-6.

Chicheley

LOCK, CAMPBELL, ed. 'Marriages at Chicheley, 1539 to 1812', in PHILLIMORE, W.P.W., ed. *B.P.R.M.* **3**, *P.P.R.S.* **71**. Phillimore, 1907, 137-55.

Cholesbury

'Marriages at Cholesbury, 1576 to 1812', in PHILLIMORE, W.P.W., & RAGG, F.W., eds. *B.P.R.M.* **1**, *P.P.R.S.* **35**. Phillimore, 1902, 17-23.

Denham

GURNEY, THOS., ed. 'Marriages at Denham, 1569 to 1812', in PHILLIMORE, W.P.W., & GURNEY, THOMAS, eds. *B.P.R.M.* **7**, *P.P.R.S.* **172**. Phillimore, 1911, 133-56.

Dorney

GURNEY, THOS., ed. 'Marriages at Dorney, 1538 to 1812', in PHILLIMORE, W.P.W., & GURNEY, THOMAS, eds. *B.P.R.M.* **5**, *P.P.R.S.* **123**. Phillimore, 1909, 133-41.

Drayton Parslow

BRADBROOK, WILLIAM, ed. *Buckinghamshire baptisms, marriages and burials, vol.II (New series): Drayton Parslow, 1559-1837*, transcribed by C.F. Clark. Chas A. Bernau for B.P.R.S., 1913.

CLARK, C.F., ed. 'Marriages at Drayton Parslow, 1559 to 1837', in PHILLIMORE, W.P.W., ed. *B.P.R.M.* **3**, *P.P.R.S.* **71**. Phillimore, 1907, 85-101.

Edgcott

See Aston Abbots

Edlesborough

'Marriages at Edlesborough, 1568 to 1812', in PHILLIMORE, W.P.W., & RAGG, F.W., eds. *B.P.R.M.* **1**, *P.P.R.S.* **35**. Phillimore, 1902, 25-61.

GROF, LASZLO. 'Edlesborough worthies', *O.* **8**(3), 1982, 85. 18th c. burials, giving occupations, etc.

Eton

'Some gleanings from the old register of the parish of Eton, Bucks', *Oxford diocesan magazine* **102**, 1910, 303-4.

Fenny Stratford

BRADBROOK, WILLIAM, ed. *The register of Saint Martin's Chapell in Fenny Stratford, Co.Buckingham, 1730-1812*. Parish Register Society **62**, 1908. Includes list of curates and vicars since 1730.

Fingest

GURNEY, THOS., ed. 'Marriages at Fingest, 1607 to 1812', in PHILLIMORE, W.P.W., & GURNEY, THOMAS, eds. *B.P.R.M.* **6**, *P.P.R.S.* **134**. Phillimore, 1910, 133-43.

Fleet Marston

'Marriages at Fleet Marston, 1677-91', *O.* **2**(3), 1978, 22-4. Includes many marriages of non-residents.

Fulmer

GURNEY, THOS., ed. 'Marriages at Fulmer, 1688 to 1812', in PHILLIMORE, W.P.W., & GURNEY, THOMAS, eds. *B.P.R.M.* **5**, *P.P.R.S.* **123**. Phillimore, 1909, 143-51.

Gayhurst

BRADBROOK, W. 'The Gayhurst register transcripts', *Genealogists magazine* **5**, 1929-31, 285-7. Brief note.

Great Brickhill

BLETCHLEY ARCHAEOLOGICAL AND HISTORICAL SOCIETY *St.Mary the Virgin, Great Brickhill, Bucks., parish registers: baptisms, 1558-1917; marriages, 1558-1982; burials, 1558-1883*. Bletchley: the Society, [1986].

Great Hampden

EBBLEWHITE, ERNEST ARTHUR, ed. *The parish registers of Great Hampden, Co.Bucks, from 1557 to 1812; also copies of the monumental inscriptions in the church and churchyard, and a full list of the successive rectors*. Mitchell and Hughes, 1888.

Great Marlow

COCKS, ALFRED HENEAGE, ed. *The earliest register of the parish of Great Marlow, Buckinghamshire, 1592-1611*. B.P.R.S. **3**. Exeter: William Pollard & Co., 1904.

Great Woolstone

BANNERMAN, W. BRUCE, ed. *The parish registers of Great Woolstone, Co.Bucks*. Transcribed by William Bradbrook. Parish Register Society **81**, 1919. 1538-1810.

Grove

TATHAM, F.H., ed. 'Marriages at Grove, 1711 to 1812', in PHILLIMORE, W.P.W., ed. *B.P.R.M.* **3**, *P.P.R.S.* **71**. Phillimore, 1907, 35-8.

Hartwell

GURNEY, F.G., ed. 'Marriages at Hartwell, 1553 to 1812', in PHILLIMORE, W.P.W., ed. *B.P.R.M.* **3**, *P.P.R.S.* **71**. Phillimore, 1907, 61-73.

Hawridge

'Marriages at Hawridge, 1600 to 1812', in PHILLIMORE, W.P.W., & RAGG, F.W., eds. *B.P.R.M.* **1**, *P.P.R.S.* **35**. Phillimore, 1902, 124-9.

Hedgerley

GURNEY, THOS., ed. 'Marriages at Hedgerley, 1539 to 1812', in PHILLIMORE, W.P.W., & GURNEY, THOMAS, eds. *B.P.R.M.* **4**, *P.P.R.S.* **96**. Phillimore, 1908, 137-56.

Hedsor

GURNEY, THOS, ed. 'Marriages at Hedsor, 1678 to 1837', in PHILLIMORE, W.P.W., & GURNEY, THOMAS, eds. *B.P.R.M.* **5**, *P.P.R.S.* **123**. Phillimore, 1909, 105-11.

High Wycombe

SUTCLIFFE, BARRY P., ed. *High Wycombe baptisms, vol.4: 1775-1812*. High Wycombe: B.F.H.S., 1992.

SUTCLIFFE, BARRY P., ed. *High Wycombe baptisms, vol.5: 1813-1837*. Haddenham: B.F.H.S., 1983. Earlier volumes are not yet (1993) published.

GURNEY, THOMAS, ed. 'Marriages at High Wycombe, 1600 to 1812', in PHILLIMORE, W.P.W., & GURNEY, THOMAS, eds. *B.P.R.M.* **6**, *P.P.R.S.* **134**. Phillimore, 1910, 1-123.

DOWNS, R.S. 'The parish church of High Wycombe (fourth notice): the parish register—introductory', *R.o.B.* **8**, 1903, 249-75. General discussion; includes brief extracts.

Hitcham

GURNEY, THOS., ed. 'Marriages at Hitcham, 1559 to 1812', in PHILLIMORE, W.P.W., & GURNEY, THOMAS, eds. *B.P.R.M.* **5**, *P.P.R.S.* **123**. Phillimore, 1909, 113-21.

Hardmead

GREEN, E.E.B., ed. 'Marriages at Hormead or Hardmead, 1575 to 1813', in PHILLIMORE, W.P.W., & RAGG, F.W., eds. *B.P.R.M.* **2**, *P.P.R.S.* **40**. Phillimore, 1904, 141-9.

Horsenden

McLAUGHLIN, E. 'Marriages at Horsenden, 1707-1836', *O.* **3**(3), 1979, 29.

Hughendon

GURNEY, THOS., ed. 'Marriages at Hughenden, 1559 to 1812', in PHILLIMORE, W.P.W., & GURNEY, THOMAS, eds. *B.P.R.M.* **7**, *P.P.R.S.* **172**. Phillimore, 1911, 1-97.

IDLE, JANET. 'The place of resort: Hughendon', *O.* **2**(2), 1978, 21-8. Index of marriages at Hughenden, 1700-21, where both parties came from other parishes. Arranged by parish.

Ibstone

GURNEY, THOMAS, ed. 'Marriages at Ibstone, 1665 to 1812', in PHILLIMORE, W.P.W., & GURNEY, THOMAS, eds. *B.P.R.M.* **6**, *P.P.R.S.* **134**. Phillimore, 1910, 145-51.

Iver

GURNEY, THOS., ed. 'Marriages at Iver, 1605 to 1812', in PHILLIMORE, W.P.W., & GURNEY, THOMAS, eds. *B.P.R.M.* **8**, *P.P.R.S.* **177**. Phillimore, 1912, 1-32.

N., J.G. 'Extracts from the parish register of Iver in Buckinghamshire', *Collectanea topographica et genealogica* **3**, 1836, 279-84.

Ivinghoe

HARVEY, T., ed. 'Marriages at Ivinghoe, 1559 to 1812', in PHILLIMORE, W.P.W., & RAGG, F.W., eds. *B.P.R.M.* **2**, *P.P.R.S.* **40**. Phillimore, 1904, 59-113. See end paper for corrigenda.

Lathbury

BALE, R.F., ed. 'Marriages at Lathbury, 1690 to 1837', in his *B.P.R.M.* **9**, *P.P.R.S.* **231**. Phillimore & Co., 1923, 131-8.

Leckhamstead

[USSHER, R.], ed. *Leckhamstead parish register.* Aylesbury: Bucks Advertiser, 1912. Reprinted from *Bucks Advertiser.* Covers 1558-1812.

Linslade

GURNEY, F.G. 'Marriages at Linslade, 1575 to 1812', in PHILLIMORE, W.P.W., ed. *B.P.R.M.* **3**, *P.P.R.S.* **71**. Phillimore, 1907, 75-84.

Little Brickhill

BLETCHLEY ARCHAEOLOGICAL AND HISTORICAL SOCIETY *St.Mary Magdalene, Little Brickhill, Bucks., parish registers: baptisms, marriages, burials, 1559-1988.* The Society, 1989.

Little Missenden

GURNEY, THOS., ed. 'Marriages at Little Missenden, 1559 to 1812', in PHILLIMORE, W.P.W., & GURNEY, THOMAS, eds. *B.P.R.M.* **7**, *P.P.R.S.* **172**. Phillimore, 1911, 99-131.

Little Woolstone

BANNERMAN, W. BRUCE, ed. *The parish registers of Little Woolstone, Co.Bucks,* transcribed by William Bradbrook. Parish Register Society **80**, 1919. 1596-1813.

Long Crendon

LEE, FREDERICK GEORGE. 'St.Mary's church, Long Crendon, Bucks', *R.o.B.* **6**, 1887, 271-95. Includes extracts from the burial register, monumental inscriptions, etc.

MOFFAT, S.E. 'The story of the old register book of Long Crendon, Bucks', *Home Counties Magazine* **6**, 1904, 181-6. General discussion.

Marsworth

'Marriages at Masworth or Marsworth, 1574 to 1812', in PHILLIMORE, W.P.W., & RAGG, F.W., eds. *B.P.R.M.* **1**, *P.P.R.S.* **35**. Phillimore, 1902, 73-81.

Medmenham

PLAISTEAD, ARTHUR HENRY. *The parsons and parish registers of Medmenham, Buckinghamshire.* Longmans Green & Co., 1932. Parish registers transcribed cover 1575-1930. Also includes notes on clergy and parish clerks, and list of churchwardens.

Mentmore

GRUBBE, C.S., ed. 'Marriages at Mentmore, 1575 to 1812', in PHILLIMORE, W.P.W., & RAGG, F.W., eds. *B.P.R.M.* **1**, *P.P.R.S.* **35**. Phillimore, 1902, 63-72.

PAREZ, C.H. *The register of the parish of Mentmore, Co.Bucks, 1685-1829.* B.P.R.S. **11**, 1909.

Moulsoe

BALE, R.F., ed. 'Marriages at Moulsoe, 1559 to 1837', in his *B.P.R.M.* **9**, *P.P.R.S.* **231**. Phillimore & Co., 1923, 147-63.

Newport Pagnell

BALE, RONALD F., ed. 'Marriages at Newport Pagnell, 1558 to 1837', in his *B.P.R.M.* **9**, *P.P.R.S.* **231**. Phillimore & Co., 1923, 1-130.
'Private burial places at Newport Pagnell', *R.o.B.* **11**, 1920-26, 88-90. Brief discussion with names.

Newton Longville

BANNERMAN, W. BRUCE, ed. *The parish registers of Newton Longville, Co.Bucks*, transcribed by William Bradbrook. Parish Register Society **53-4**, 1922. 1560-1840.

BRADBROOK, W. 'Newton Longville parish register', *R.o.B.* **11**, 1920-26, 121-9. General discussion, with list of frequently occurring surnames.

Olney

RATCLIFF, OLIVER, ed. *The register of the parish of Olney, Co.Bucks., 1665 to 1812*. B.P.R.S. **6, 7, 10, 12 & 13**, [1907-10].

Pitstone

'Marriages at Pitstone, 1576 to 1812', in PHILLIMORE, W.P.W., & RAGG, F.W., eds. *B.P.R.M.* **1**, *P.P.R.S.* **35**. Phillimore, 1902, 131-45.

Princes Risborough

McLAUGHLIN, EVE. *Princes Risborough Baptist Chapel: births, 1796-1837; list of members, 1797-1840* transcribed by Rex Kidd. B.F.H.S., 1987. Reprinted Haddenham: Buckinghamshire Publications, 1990.

Ravenstone

RATCLIFF, OLIVER, ed. *The register of the parish of Ravenstone, Co.Bucks, 1568 to 1812*. B.P.R.S. **14**, [1911].

Saint Leonard

'Marriages at St.Leonard's, Aston Clinton, 1739 to 1812', in PHILLIMORE, W.P.W., ed. *B.P.R.M.* **3**, *P.P.R.S.* **71**. Phillimore, 1907, 103-7.

Sherington

LOCK, CAMPBELL, ed. 'Marriages at Sherington, 1698 to 1812', in PHILLIMORE, W.P.W., ed. *B.P.R.M.* **3**, *P.P.R.S.* **71**. Phillimore, 1907, 109-23.

Slapton

'Marriages at Slapton, 1653 to 1812', in PHILLIMORE, W.P.W., & RAGG, F.W., eds. *B.P.R.M.* **1**, *P.P.R.S.* **35**. Phillimore, 1902, 83-9.

Soulbury

'Marriages at Soulbury, 1575 to 1812', in PHILLIMORE, W.P.W., & RAGG, F.W., eds. *B.P.R.M.* **1**, *P.P.R.S.* **35**. Phillimore, 1902, 91-121.

Stewkley

DICKSON, R. BRUCE, ed. *Parish register of Stewkeley, Buckinghamshire, England, 1545-1643*. Salem, Mass: Eben Putnam, 1897. Reprinted from *Putnam's Monthly Historical Magazine* **4**(1), 1896.
'Marriages at Stewkley, 1813-1822', *O.* **3**(4), 1979, 25-6.

Stoke Poges

GURNEY, THOS., ed. 'Marriages at Stoke Poges, 1563 to 1812', in PHILLIMORE, W.P.W., & GURNEY, THOMAS, eds. *B.P.R.M.* **4**, *P.P.R.S.* **96**. Phillimore, 1908, 157-84.

REYNOLDS, E. LIONEL, ed. *The register of the parish of Stoke Poges, in the County of Buckingham, 1563-1653*. B.P.R.S. **9 & 16**, [1908]-12.

Stone

GURNEY, FREDERICK G., ed. 'Marriages at Stone, 1538 to 1812', in PHILLIMORE, W.P.W., ed. *B.P.R.M.* **3**, *P.P.R.S.* **71**. Phillimore, 1907, 39-60.

Swanbourne

USSHER, R., ed. *The parish register of Swanbourne, Co.Bucks., from October 18th, 1565 to December 31st, 1836*. Buckingham: Marsh & Co., 1915. Includes list of vicars, etc.

McLAUGHLIN, EVE, ed. *Swanbourne Baptist Chapel: births register, membership lists and connecting data from parish registers*. 2nd ed. Haddenham: Buckinghamshire Publications, 1993.

Taplow

GURNEY, THOS., ed. 'Marriages at Taplow, 1710 to 1812', in PHILLIMORE, W.P.W., & GURNEY, THOMAS, eds. *B.P.R.M.* **5**, *P.P.R.S.* **123**. Phillimore, 1909, 123-31.

Thornton

DAWSON-SMITH, C.C., ed. *The register of the parish of Thornton in the County of Buckinghamshire, 1562-1812*. Parish Register Society **2**. Exeter: William Pollard & Co., 1903.

Turville

GRAVES, MICHAEL, ed. 'Marriages at Turville, 1583 to 1812', in PHILLIMORE, W.P.W., & GURNEY, THOMAS, eds. *B.P.R.M.* **6**, *P.P.R.S.* **134**. Phillimore, 1910, 153-61.

Upton

REYNOLDS, E. LIONEL. 'Upton-cum-Chalvey parish register', *R.o.B.* **9**, 1909, 179-93. General discussion, with brief extracts.

Walton

BRADBROOK, WILLIAM, ed. *The register of the parish of Walton (near Bletchley), Buckinghamshire, 1598-1812.* B.P.R.S. **1**, 1901.

Wavendon

BRADBROOK, WILLIAM. 'Wavendon', *R.o.B.* **9**, 1909, 31-53. General discussion of the parish register, with some extracts.

Wendover

'Marriages at Wendover, 1576 to 1812', in PHILLIMORE, W.P.W., & RAGG, F.W., eds. *B.P.R.M.* **2**, *P.P.R.S.* **40**. Phillimore, 1904, 1-58.

Westbury

USSHER, R. *A history of the parish of Westbury in the County of Buckingham.* [ ]: [the author], 1905. Reprinted from the *Buckingham Advertiser.* Includes transcript of the parish register, 1550-1849, monumental inscriptions and abstracts of 150+ deeds, etc.

USSHER, R. 'Marriages at Westbury, 1558 to 1837', in PHILLIMORE, W.P.W., ed. *B.P.R.M.* **3**, *P.P.R.S.* **71**. Phillimore, 1907, 125-36.

Weston Underwood

CRISP, FREDERICK ARTHUR, ed. *Catholic registers of Weston Underwood in the County of Buckingham.* F.A. Crisp, 1887. 18th c.

'Springs and roundabouts, or, you can't win them all', *Catholic ancestor* **3**(1), 1990, 31. List of converts, 1710-19, from the Catholic registers of Weston Underwood, Bucks.

Wing

TATHAM, FRANCIS HENRY, ed. 'Marriages at Wing, 1546 to 1812', in PHILLIMORE, W.P.W., ed. *B.P.R.M.* **3**, *P.P.R.S.* **71**. Phillimore, 1907, 1-34.

WOODMAN, A. VERE, ed. *The register of the parish of Wing, Buckinghamshire, 1546-1812.* 2 vols. B.P.R.S. **18** & **19**, 1914-15.

Wooburn

GURNEY, THOS., ed. 'Marriages at Wooburn, 1653 to 1812', in PHILLIMORE, W.P.W., & GURNEY, THOMAS, eds. *B.P.R.M.* **5**, *P.P.R.S.* **123**. Phillimore, 1909, 69-103.

Woughton on the Green

BRADBROOK, WILLIAM. *The register of the parish of Woughton on the Green in the County of Buckinghamshire, 1558 to [1812].* B.P.R.S. **5** & **8**, [1906-8].

8. PROBATE RECORDS

Probate records—wills, inventories, administration bonds, etc.—are invaluable sources of genealogical information. In order to use them, an appreciation of the administrative structure of the probate courts is necessary. For Buckinghamshire, this is provided by:

GIBSON, JEREMY. 'Probate jurisdiction before 1858', *O.* **2**(2), 1978, 11-12.

The most important probate court for Buckinghamshire was that of the Archdeaconry of Buckingham. The early wills amongst the Archdeaconry records are discussed in:

ELVEY, ELIZABETH M. 'Early records of the Archdeaconry of Buckingham: their importance to the social historian', *R.o.B.* **19**, 1971-4, 55-61.

Some 250 wills are abstracted in:

ELVEY, E.M., ed. *The courts of the Archdeaconry of Buckingham, 1483-1523.* B.R.S. **19**, 1975.

See also:

RAGG, F.W. 'A record of the Archdeaconry courts of Buckingham during part of 1521', *R.o.B.* **10**, 1916, 304-31. Includes many proofs of wills; also much other litigation.

A few Buckinghamshire wills are included in:

GIBBONS, ALFRED. *Early Lincoln wills: an abstract of all the wills and administrations recorded in the episcopal registers of the old diocese of Lincoln, comprising the counties of Lincoln, Rutland, Northampton, Huntingdon, Bedford, Buckingham, Oxford, Leicester and Hertford, 1280-1547.* Lincoln: James Williamson, 1888.

CHEYNE, ERNEST, & BARRATT, D.M., eds. *Probate records of the courts of the Bishop and Archdeacon of Oxford, 1516-1732.* 2 vols. Index Library **93-4**. British Record Society, 1985-5. Index only

Many Buckinghamshire testators proved their wills in the Prerogative Court of Canterbury, and reference should be made to the indexes etc. cited in *English genealogy: an introductory bibliography*, section 11. See also:

'P.C.C. wills', *O.* **7**(4), 1983, 117. List, 1686-93, of Buckinghamshire testators from the printed indexes.

Many probate inventories are printed in:

REED, MICHAEL, ed. *Buckinghamshire probate inventories, 1661-1714.* B.R.S. **24**, 1988.

Probate records *continued*

Other works of interest include:

BROWNE, A.L. 'Wills of Buckinghamshire clergy in the sixteenth century', *R.o.B.* **13**, 1934-40, 195-204. Wills of Richard Halley, 1520, Robert Fleming, 1526, Richard Rathbone, 1522, and Percival Duvall, 1528.

CLEAR, A.J. 'Notes on the four Buckinghamshire parishes in the Archdeaconry of St.Albans', *R.o.B.* **12**, 1927-33, 24-28. Lists 15th c. wills and clergy for Aston Abbots, Little Horwood, Granborough and Winslow.

CHESS VALLEY ARCHAEOLOGICAL & HISTORICAL SOCIETY *A catalogue of wills, charters, maps ... illustrating the recorded history of Chesham, as part of the Chesham One Thousand Exhibition.* Chesham: the Society, 1970.

SHRIMPTON, RAY. 'The Gurney will books', *O.* **16**(4), 1992, 155-6. Lists 300+ names; draws attention to a useful collection of wills.

Many wills, etc., of particular individuals or families have been printed. See:

Bodington

'Bodington wills, etc.', *M.G.H.* 2nd series **4**, 1892, 102-4. 17-18th c.

Brudenell

'Piety and frugality', *R.o.B.* **13**, 1934-40, 427-31. Will of Joan Brudenell, 1469.

Carter

CORNWALL, JULIAN. 'John Carter of Denham, yeoman', *R.o.B.* **16**(2), 1955-6, 83-94. Based on his 1634-5 will and inventory.

Carswalle

WOODMAN, A. VERE. 'The goods of a sixteenth-century parson', *R.o.B.* **15**, 1947, 311-13. Inventory of Sir Antony Carswalle, 1521.

Gilbert

'Some yeomen's wills', *R.o.B.* **13**, 1934-40, 25-31. Gilbert family; includes pedigree, 17-18th c.

Hampden

SAWTELL, G.H. 'Notes on four inventories of goods of members of the families of Hampden and Lee of Hartwell', *R.o.B.* **3**, 1870, 3-7. 16-17th c. probate inventories.

Hore

THOMPSON, HAROLD. 'The best will in the world', *O.* **6**(1), 1982, 24-5. Extracts from the wills of John Hore of Cuddington, 1688, and Robert Hore of Dinton, 1689.

Ingilton

LAMBORN, E.A. GREENING. 'A discovery at Thornton', *R.o.B.* **15**, 1947, 46-50. Ingilton family brass, 15th c. Includes pedigree and plates.

Janes

JANES, DAVID RICHARD. 'The blacksmiths legacy', *O.* **8**(1), 1984, 26-7. Will of Joseph Janes, 1796.

Lee

See Hampden

Purefoy

'A funeral in 1765', *R.o.B.* **12**, 1927-33, 261-4. Description of monument to Mrs Purefoy.

'A sixteenth century will', *R.o.B.* 12, 1927-33, 119-24. Will of John Purefoy, 1579.

Theed

WOODMAN, A. VERE. 'Seventeenth century inventory at Crofton', *R.o.B.* **14**, 1941-6, 354-60. Will and inventory of William Theed, 1680.

White

WHITE, A.S. 'A Buckinghamshire inventory, 1703', *Home Counties Magazine* **12**, 1910, 174-7. Probate inventory of Thomas White of Monks Risborough, 1703.

9. MONUMENTAL INSCRIPTIONS

A. *GENERAL*

Monumental inscriptions are an important source of genealogical information, and many have been transcribed, especially in recent years—although most transcriptions remain unpublished. A list of transcripts existing in 1914 is printed in:
'Buckinghamshire churchyard inscriptions', *Register of English monumental inscriptions* **2**, 1914, 26-31.

A number of surveys of particular types of monuments are available; see:

ESDAILE, KATHARINE A. 'The Renaissance monuments of Buckinghamshire', *R.o.B.* **15**, 1947, 32-45.

KELKE, W. HASTINGS. 'The sculptured monuments of Buckinghamshire prior to the sixteenth century', *R.o.B.* **3**, 1870, 8-23.

BOODLE, J.A. 'The sepulchral brasses of Buckinghamshire', *R.o.B.* **2**, 1863, 254-6, 293-8; **3**, 1870, 106-19 & 165-8. Incomplete.

SANDERSON, H.K.ST.J. 'Notes on the brasses in some Buckinghamshire churches', *Transactions of the Monumental Brass Society* **3**, 1897-9, 115-8; **4**, 1900-1903, 31-6 & 165-76. See also 246-9.

BADHAM, SALLY, & BLAIR, JOHN. 'Some lost Buckinghamshire brasses recorded by Browne Willis', *Transactions of the Monumental Brass Society* **13**, 1980, 25-9. Brief note.

SUMMERS, PETER, ed. *Hatchments in Britain, 4: Bedfordshire, Berkshire, Buckinghamshire, Oxfordshire and Wiltshire.* Phillimore, 1983.

LAMBORN, E.A. GREENING. *The armorial glass of the Oxford Diocese, 1250-1850.* O.U.P., for the Berkshire Archaeological Society, 1949. Berkshire, Buckinghamshire and Oxfordshire.

LAMBORN, E.A. GREENING. 'The armorial glass of the Oxford Diocese', *Berkshire Archaeological Journal* **46**, 1942, 45-53 & 88-96; **47**, 1943, 24-45.

LAMBORN, E.A. GREENING. 'The armorial fonts of the Oxford Diocese', *Berkshire Archaeological Journal* **45**, 1941, 106-19; **46**, 1942, 32-4.

IMPERIAL WAR GRAVES COMMISSION *The War Graves of the British Empire: the register of the names of those who fell in the Great War and are buried in cemeteries and churchyards in the administrative county of Buckingham.* Imperial War Graves Commission, 1930.

COMMONWEALTH WAR GRAVES COMMISSION *The War dead of the Commonwealth: the register of the names of those who fell in the 1939-45 war and are buried in cemeteries and churchyards in the counties of Bedfordshire and Buckinghamshire.* Commonwealth War Graves Commission, 1961.

B. *BY PLACE*

Bletchley
BRADBROOK, WILLIAM. 'Bletchley monuments and epitaphs', *R.o.B.* **9**, 1909, 194-207. Includes pedigree of Jauncey, 17-19th c.

Chalfont St.Giles
CLARKE, H. ADAMS. *Chalfont St.Giles: a history of the parish church of St.Giles.* Beaconsfield: the author, 1961. Includes notes on brasses, hatchments, registers, clergy and churchwardens, etc.

Chalfont St.Peter
WOODS, F.H. 'Chalfont St.Peters', *Home Counties Magazine* **1**, 1899, 131-6. Includes a few monumental inscriptions.

Chenies
BEDFORD, ADELINE MARIE. *Chenies church and monuments.* Chiswick Press, 1901.

Clifton Reynes
KELKE, W. HASTINGS. 'On three sepulchral monuments at Clifton Reynes, in the County of Buckingham', *Archaeological journal* **11**, 1854, 149-56.

Denham
OSWALD-HICKS, T.W. 'Inscriptions from the churchyard of St.Mary, Denham, in the Hundred of Stoke in the County of Buckingham, 1912', *Registry of English monumental inscriptions* **1**, 1912, 62-8.

Dinton
RUTTER, DAVID C. 'Palimpsest brasses at Dinton', *R.o.B.* **15**, 1947, 153-65.

RUTTER, DAVID C. 'Palimpsest brasses at Dinton, Buckinghamshire', *Transactions of the Monumental Brass Society* **8**, 1943-51, 270-88.

Edlesborough
See Penn

Eton College
HARWOOD, T. 'Monumental brasses at Eton College, Bucks', *Oxford journal of monumental brasses* **2**, 1900, 11-28 & 68-85.

Fenny Stratford

BRADBROOK, WILLIAM. 'Armorial ceiling at Fenny Stratford church', *R.o.B.* **8**, 1903, 374-402. Lists 75 arms.

Fenny Stratford cemetery, Bucks: memorial inscriptions. Bletchley Archaeological and Historical Society, [198-?].

Fingest

OSWALD-HICKS, T.W. 'The monumental inscriptions within the church of St.Bartholomew, Fingest, in the Hundred of Desborough (Dunstenburgh) in the County of Buckingham, 1913', *Register of English monumental inscriptions* **2**, 1914, 11-19. Also in churchyard.

Great Hampden

RUTTER, D.C. 'Palimpsest brasses at Great Hampden, Buckinghamshire', *Transactions of the Monumental Brass Society* **9**, 1952-62, 17-26.

Great Linford

BODDINGTON, REGINALD STEWART. 'Monumental inscriptions in Great Linford church, Bucks', *M.G.H.* 2nd series **2**, 1888, 191-2.

Great Marlow

COCKS, ALFRED HENEAGE. 'The intra-mural monuments and other inscriptions of Gt.Marlow church', *R.o.B.* **8**, 1903, 162-203.

STEPHENSON, MILL. 'Monumental brasses formerly in Great Marlow church', *R.o.B.* **8**, 1903, 446-56.

Great Woolstone

BRADBROOK, W. 'Monumental inscriptions within the church of Holy Trinity, Great Woolstone, in the Hundred of Newport in the County of Buckingham', *Register of English monumental inscriptions* **2**, 1914, 20-23. Also in churchyard.

Haddenham

LEE, FREDERICK GEORGE. 'The church of St.Mary the Virgin, Haddenham', *R.o.B.* **6**, 1887, 9-26. Includes monumental inscriptions, parish register extracts, and a list of vicars.

High Wycombe

DOWNS, R.S. 'High Wycombe parish church, part II: brasses, monuments and inscriptions', *R.o.B.* **7**, 1897, 430-61. Includes pedigrees of Petty, 17-19th c., and Welles, 17-19th c.

'They rest away from their origins', *O.* **16**(2), 1992, 75. List of strays found in a transcript of monumental inscriptions for High Wycombe.

Little Missenden

'The monumental inscriptions within the church of St.John Baptist, Little Missenden, in the Hundred of Aylesbury in the County of Buckingham, 1912', *Register of English monumental inscriptions* **2**, 1914, 55-78. Reprinted from Lipscomb's *History* .... Includes churchyard; with pedigree of Olliff, 18-19th c.

Little Woolstone

BRADBROOK, W. 'Monumental inscriptions within the church of Holy Trinity, Little Woolstone, in the Hundred of Newport, in the County of Buckingham', *Register of English monumental inscriptions* **2**, 1914, 24-5. Also in churchyard.

Loughton

MYNARD, D.C. 'The wall monuments in Loughton church', *Wolverton & District Archaeological Society newsletter* **10**, 1966, 20-22.

Marsworth

STEPHENSON, MILL. 'Note on two palimpsest brasses at Marsworth', *R.o.B.* **10**, 1916, 217-23. Reprinted from *Transactions of the Monumental Brass Society*, with additions.

Middle Claydon

NORRIS, MALCOLM. 'Palimpsest finds at Middle Claydon, Bucks', *Transactions of the Monumental Brass Society* **11**, 1969-74, 463-7.

Penn

EVANS, H.F. OWEN. 'Brasses at Penn and Edlesborough', *R.o.B.* **16**(2), 1955-6, 106-9.

GRAINGER, J. 'Penn church', *R.o.B.* **5**, 1878, 271-7. Includes some monumental inscriptions.

Soulbury

LOVETT, R.J. ARDEN. 'Soulbury church, Bucks, with its monuments', *B.B.O.A.J.* **3**, 1897, 23-8.

Stoke Hammond

BRADBROOK, W. 'The monumental inscriptions within the church of St.Luke, Stoke Hamond, in the Hundred of Newport, in the County of Buckingham, 1913', *Register of English monumental inscriptions* **2**, 1914, 115-26. Includes churchyard.

Stoke Mandeville

DELL, ALAN. 'In Mandeville meadows', *O.* **5**(1), 1981, 26-7. Stoke Mandeville monumental inscriptions.

Thornton

RUSSELL, R.H. 'The monuments at Thornton, Bucks', *R.o.B.* **7**, 1897, 52-60.

Turville

COCKS, ALFRED HENEAGE. 'The intra-mural monuments of Turville church', *R.o.B.* **8**, 1903, 360-73. Includes pedigrees (one folded) of D'Oyley, 14-18th c., and Perry, 18-19th c.

Twyford

STEPHENSON, MILL. 'Notes on a palimpsest brass at Twyford', *R.o.B.* **9**, 1909, 323-8.

Walton

BRADBROOK, W. 'The monumental inscriptions within the church of St.Michael, Walton, in the Hundred of Newport in the County of Buckingham, 1909', *Register of English monumental inscriptions* **2**, 1914, 79-85. Also churchyard.

Woughton on the Green

BRADBROOK, W. 'Monumental inscriptions within the church at Woughton-on-the-Green, in the Hundred of Newport in the County of Buckingham, 1909', *Register of English monumental inscriptions* **1**, 1912, 69-70.

BRADBROOK, W. 'Inscriptions from the churchyard at Woughton-on-the-Green', *Register of English monumental inscriptions* **1**, 1912, 71-7.

Wraysbury

ROUSE, E. CLIVE. 'Armorial glass from Place Farm, Wyrardisbury, now at Fulmer Grange', *R.o.B.* **15**, 1947, 212-15. Includes pedigree showing relationship of Gobion, Paynell, Kennesman, Stonor, etc., 16th c.?

'Monumental inscriptions in the church of Wyrardisbury, lr. Wraysbury, Co.Bucks., and a pedigree of Hassel of that place', *Collectanea topographica et genealogica* **8**, 1843, 400-5. Includes pedigree of Hassell, 18-19th c.

C. *BY FAMILY*

Barker

'Barker of Great Horwood, Bucks., and of Newbury, Berks', *M.G.H.* 3rd series **3**, 1900, 198-202. Monumental inscriptions; includes 18th c. pedigree.

Bellingham

COCKS, ALFRED HENEAGE. 'A palimpsest brass at Middle Claydon', *R.o.B.* **7**, 1897, 529-30. To Walter Bellingham, 1476-7.

Brudenell

See Drury

Cave

COALES, JOHN. 'A palimpsest discovery at Chicheley, Bucks', *Transactions of the Monumental Brass Society* **9**, 1961, 438-46. Cave family monuments, 16-17th c.

Chapman

RUTTER, DAVID C. 'A palimpsest at Little Missenden, Bucks', *Transactions of the Monumental Brass Society* **8**, 1943-51, 34-6. William and Alice Chapman, 1446.

Dormer

HEMP, W.J. 'The Dormer tombs at Wing, Bucks', *Transactions of the Monumental Brass Society* **6**, 1910-14, 59-74.

Drury

BENNELL, JOHN E.G. 'A lost Chalfont St.Giles memorial brass', *R.o.B.* **17**(2), 1962, 189-91. Concerns Drury and Brudenell memorials.

Dynham

COCKS, ALFRED HENEAGE. 'Description of the brass of Roger Dynham', *R.o.B.* **7**, 1897, 262-3. 1490.

Fettiplace

DUNLOP, J. RENTON. 'Brasses commemorative of the Fettiplace family', *Transactions of the Monumental Brass Society* **6**(2), 1911, 95-119. In Berkshire, Buckinghamshire, Oxfordshire and Sussex.

Franklyn

LAMBORN, E.A. GREENING. 'Chearsley, Bucks', *Transactions of the Monumental Brass Society* **7**, 1934-42, 185-7. John and Margaret Franklyn, 15th c.

Grey

KING, THOMAS WILLIAM. 'Observations on the monumental inscription to Richard Grey, Lord Grey de Wilton, in the chapel of Eton College, Bucks', *Archaeologia* **32**, 1847, 58-9. 1521; includes pedigree, 14-16th c.

Grimsdell

'Remarkable burials', *R.o.B.* **2**, 1863, 144-9. Letters regarding the Grimsdell family monumental inscription.

Ingylton

LAMBORN, E.A. GREENING. 'The Ingylton tomb at Thornton, Bucks', *Transactions of the Monumental Brass Society* **8**, 1943-51, 186-91. 1472.

Lovett

LOVETT, R.J.A. *Ecclesiastical memorials of the Lovett family*. Ostend: A. Van de Water, 1897. Also of various other counties.

Mascoll

CARR-GOMM, F.C. 'Eustace Mascoll: brass in Farnham Royal church', *R.o.B.* **10**, 1916, 390-92. 1568.

Pygott

EVANS, H.F.O. 'The Pygott brass at Whaddon, Bucks', *Transactions of the Monumental Brass Society* **9**(1), 1952, 1-8. Thomas Pygott, 1519.

Reynes

BERRILL, N.J. 'The Reynes monuments and their possible implications for local genealogy', *R.o.B.* **22**, 1980, 105-24. Includes pedigree, medieval.

SHEPARD, GEORGE. 'Shields from Clifton Reynes', *Ancestor* **11**, 1904, 90-96. Of the Reynes family.

Russell

FRYER, ALFRED C. 'A monumental effigy of Bridget, Countess of Bedford', *Archaeological journal* **73**, 1916, 212-6. At Chenies; Russell family.

SCHARF, GEORGE, et al. *A descriptive and historical account of the Russell monuments in the Bedford Chapel at Chenies, with notices of other family monuments at Swyre, Watford, Thornhaugh, Bisham and Westminster Abbey.* Spottiswood & Co., 1892.

Saunders

SANDERSON, H.K.ST.J. 'The Saunders brasses at Pottessgrove, Beds and Wavendon, Bucks', *Transactions of the Monumental Brass Society* **2**, 1892-6, 6-9. Includes list of other Saunders brasses.

Verney

STONE, LAWRENCE. 'The Verney tomb at Middle Claydon', *R.o.B.* **16**(2), 1955-6, 67-82. 17th c.

Whitelock

HEAD, LORNA M. 'The Whitelock monument in Farley church', *R.o.B.* **26**, 1984, 117-23. See also **27**, 1985, [ii]. 1633.

10. OFFICIAL LISTS OF NAMES

Genealogists love governments which list their subjects. Official lists of names have been compiled for a multitude of reasons; those which concern us here include taxation, loyalty, the census, the defence of the realm, and the franchise. The earliest such list was, of course, Domesday, which is readily available in a modern edition:

MORRIS, JOHN, ed. *Domesday book, 13: Buckinghamshire*. Chichester: Phillimore, 1978.

Taxation Lists

The records of taxation are an important source for identifying ancestors, and for Buckinghamshire a number of major tax lists have been published. They are listed here in chronological order for the county, followed by a brief list of returns for specific places.

CHIBNALL, A.C. *Early taxation returns: taxation of personal property in 1332 and later.* B.R.S. **14**, 1966. In addition to the 1332 tax, this includes the carucage of 1217, assessments of Horton and Stone, 1336, and of Emberton, 1512/13, a few returns of 1327, etc.

CHIBNALL, A.C., & WOODMAN, A. VERE, eds. *Subsidy roll for the County of Buckingham, anno 1524.* B.R.S. **8**, 1950 (for 1944).

SALTER, HERBERT EDWARD, ed. *A subsidy collected in the Diocese of Lincoln in 1526.* Oxford: Historical Society **63**, 1909. Includes Buckinghamshire; clergy names only.

RAGG, F.W. 'Schedule of tenths and fifteenths of the Archdeaconry of Buckingham', *R.o.B.* **10**, 1916, 403-34. For index, see 455-7. Tax list for the clergy, c.1529.

'The names of those persons who subscribed towards the defence of this country at the time of the Spanish Armada and the amount they contributed: from the County of Buckingham', *O.* **1**(1), 1976, 9-10.

BONSEY, CAROL G., & JENKINS, J.G., eds. *Ship money papers and Richard Grenville's note-book.* B.R.S. **13**, 1965. Of the 1620s and 1630s; includes lists of taxpayers.

WILSON, JOHN, ed. *Buckinghamshire contributions for Ireland, and Richard Grenville's military accounts, 1642-45.* B.R.S. **21**, 1983.

GIBSON, J.S.W. 'Tax records for the reign of Charles II in the Bucks Record Office', *O.* **9**(3), 1985, 87. Brief note.

Burnham Hundred

'The account of subscriptions to the present to King Charles II from the Hundred of Burnham', *R.o.B.* **7**, 1897, 71-4. 1661 tax list.

Great Hampden

DAVIES, LESLEY WYNNE. 'The taxman cometh', *O.* **9**(2), 1985, 61-3. Great Hampden tax lists: 1660 poll tax, 1668 and 1673 aids.

Stone

GURNEY, FREDK. G. 'A fourteenth century subsidy for Stone', *R.o.B.* **10**, 1916, 224-7. 1335-7.

Oaths of Allegiance

Loyalty to the Crown was an important matter in the unsettled state of seventeenth and eighteenth century England. Consequently, oaths of loyalty were administered on a number of occasions, and recorded for posterity. A number of publications have resulted:

GANDY, WALLACE. 'The Association Oath rolls for Buckinghamshire, A.D. 1696', *R.o.B.* **11**, 1920-26, 109-20. General discussion, with transcript of roll for Stone, etc.

LE HARDY, WILLIAM, ed. *Calendar of Quarter Sessions records vol. VI: lists of persons who took oaths of allegiance, etc., and Quakers who affirmed, 1723-24; register of estates of Roman Catholics, 1717-48.* Aylesbury: Clerk of the Peace, 1953.

ANDREWS, ARCHIBALD. 'Buckland', *O.* **8**(3), 1984, 71-3. Brief history, including list of those who took the oath of allegiance to George I in 1723, and a list of bridegrooms, 1760-79.

McLAUGHLIN, EVE. 'Edlesborough worthies', *O.* **6**(3), 1982, 64. List of those taking the oath of loyalty to George I, 1723.

Muster Rolls and Militia Lists

The defence of the realm necessitated the involvement of everyone fit to bear arms, i.e. every adult male. Consequently, muster rolls provide comprehensive listings of adult males, and identify almost every family in the county. Two sixteenth century rolls are in print:

CHIBNALL, A.C., ed. *The certificate of musters for Buckinghamshire in 1522.* B.R.S. **17**, 1973. Also published as HISTORICAL MANUSCRIPTS COMMISSION *J[oint] P[ublication]* **18**.

BALDWIN, ROLLAND T., ed. *The certificate of musters for Buckinghamshire 1535.* Melbourne Beach, Florida: the editor, 1989.

A general discussion of the militia at a later period, with useful references, is provided by:

BECKETT, IAN F.W. 'The evolution and decline of the Restoration militia in Buckinghamshire, 1660-1745', *R.o.B.* **26**, 1984, 28-43.

See also:

BECKETT, I.F.W. 'Buckinghamshire militia lists for 1759: a social analysis', *R.o.B.* **20**, 1975-8, 461-5.

'Militia enrolments and substitutes', *O.* **16**(3), 1992, 108-10. Militia lists for the hundreds of Desborough and Aylesbury (part), 1759.

'Militia enrolments and substitutes', *O.* **16**(2), 1992, 71-4. Militia lists for the Hundreds of Buckingham and Cottesloe, 1759.

A full list of the militia at the end of the eighteenth century—which is virtually a listing of every able bodied man in the county—is provided by:

BECKETT, IAN F., ed. *The Buckinghamshire posse comitatus, 1798.* B.R.S. **22**, 1985. This is discussed in:

McLAUGHLIN, EVE. 'The posse comitatus, 1798', *O.* **10**(1), 1986, 30-32.

'The able men of Fenny Stratford, 1798', *O.* **3**(1), 1979, 21. Presumably a militia list, giving names and occupations.

Poll Books

Eighteenth and nineteenth-century poll books list those claiming the right to vote, and show how their votes were exercised. Full details of these cannot be given here; consult the works listed in *English genealogy: an introductory bibliography*, section 12D. Modern works include:

Before the Reform Act: elections in Buckinghamshire, 1740-1832. [2nd ed.] Archive teaching unit **2**. Aylesbury: Buckinghamshire Record Office, [1991]. Includes extracts from poll books.

CHORLTON, NICK. 'Stoke Mandeville electors in 1868', *O.* **5**(3), 1981, 21-2. List of those entitled to vote for Aylesbury M.P's.

The Census

By far the most useful official lists are the census enumerators' schedules of the 19th century. Works on these are listed here chronologically. First, however, a private census of 1760 must be mentioned.

1760

McLAUGHLIN, EVE, ed. *The West Wycombe census 1760: a list of householders and their families.* Haddenham: Buckinghamshire Publications, 1993. Also includes the posse comitatus, 1798 (listing adult males).

1821 & 1831

McLAUGHLIN, EVE, ed. *The Princes Risborough censuses of 1821 and 1831*. Haddenham: Buckinghamshire Publications, 1992. Transcript.

1841

McLAUGHLIN, EVE, ed. *The Workhouse population of Buckinghamshire in 1841*, transcribed by Bertrand Shrimpton. Haddenham: Buckinghamshire Publications, 1992. Transcript of workhouse census schedules; includes out of county unions with Buckinghamshire parishes.

1851

CROWTON, PETER. 'Bucks migrants to the Derby mills', *O.* **9**(1), 1985, 31-2. From 1851 census of Padfield, Derbyshire.

1851 census: P.R.O. piece HO.107 1723: surname index. [Bletchley]: Bletchley Archaeological and Historial Society, [1990?]. Covers most of North Buckinghamshire, i.e. the Newport Hundreds.

Aylesbury

RALPH, NORMAN. *1851 census transcript and surname index: Aylesbury PRO: HO107/1721*. B.F.H.S., 1991.

McLAUGHLIN, E. 'Guests of Her Majesty the Queen', *O.* **7**(2), 1983, 52-4. See also **7**(3), 1983, 67. Lists 164 inmates of Aylesbury gaol, from the 1851 census.

Beaconsfield

ABBOTT, ERIC. *Transcription of the 1851 census of the parish of Beaconsfield, Bucks.* [ ]: B.F.H.S., 1988.

Bledlow

PRYER, WALTER. 'The Bledlow migrants to the North', *O.* **7**(3), 1983, 114-5. Extracts from 1851 census returns for Lancashire and Cheshire.

Brill

'The Methodist connexion', *O.* **8**(3), 1984, 74. See also **8**(4), 1984, 97. List of resident staff and pupils at Brill Methodist school for girls, from the 1851 census.

Haddenham

McLAUGHLIN, EVE. 'The inhabitants of Haddenham, 1851', *O.* **5**(1), 1981, 24-5. Gives names and occupations only from the 1851 census.

Lacey Green

KINGHAM, C., & McLAUGHLIN, EVE, eds. *Lacey Green and Loosley Row, 1851*. Haddenham: Buckinghamshire Publications, 1992. Census transcript.

Longwick

McLAUGHLIN, EVE, ed. *Longwick census 1851*. Haddenham: Buckinghamshire Publications, 1991. Transcript.

Marlow

McLAUGHLIN, EVE. *Marlow inhabitants in 1851: street listing of householders and other surnames; directory, gentry and commercial; electors and tenants*. Haddenham: Buckinghamshire Publications, 1992. From the census, Slater's directory, and a voters list.

Newport Pagnell

McLAUGHLIN, EVE. 'The inhabitants of Newport Pagnell workhouse, 1851', *O.* **10**(4), 1986, 135-9. From the census.

Princes Risborough

Princes Risborough, 1851. 2nd ed. Haddenham: Buckinghamshire Publications, 1992. Census transcript.

Winslow

McLAUGHLIN, EVE, ed. *Winslow census 1851*. Haddenham: Buckinghamshire Publications, 1993. Transcript.

Wootton Underwood

McLAUGHLIN, EVE, ed. *Wootton Underwood 1851-81*, transcribed by D. Purslow. Haddenham: Buckinghamshire Publications, 1992. Census transcript and index.

1861

Princes Risborough

QUICK, B.O. *Princes Risborough 1861 index*. Haddenham: Buckinghamshire Publications, 1993.

Wolverton

FRENCH, J. 'Wolverton: a magnet for migrants, 1837-1861', *R.o.B.* **28**, 1986, 138-47. Based on the 1861 census.

See also 1851

1871

McL[AUGHLIN], E. 'Marlow Place School, 1871', *O.* **8**(4), 1985, 114. Staff and pupils in the 1871 census.

McLAUGHLIN, EVE. 'Scholars at Marlow, 1871', *O.* **9**(1), 1985, 35. From the census; for a school in St.Peters Street.

'The Cliveden set', *O.* **9**(2), 1985, 57-60. Lists residents in the 1871 census, including members of the Grosvenor family, their guests, and many staff.

See also 1851

1881

The Mormons are currently finalising a complete index of the 1881 census. Until this is available, see:

McLAUGHLIN, EVE. 'Sick, sick and very very sick', *O.* **14**(2), 1990, 105. 1881 census, Royal Bucks Infirmary.

'A better class of orphan', *O.* **14**(4), 1990, 134-6. 1881 census for the British Orphan Asylum at Slough.

See also 1851

Landowners

A different type of census was taken in 1873. Everyone who owned more than one acre of land was listed, and the returns were published in the Parliamentary papers series. See:

'Buckinghamshire', in *Return of owners of land, 1873* vol.1. C.1097. H.M.S.O., 1875.

11. DIRECTORIES AND MAPS

Directories are invaluable sources of information for locating people in the past. For the nineteenth century, they are the equivalent of the modern phone book. Many directories for Buckinghamshire were published. The following list is selective, based mainly on volumes actually seen in Aylesbury and London, although also drawing on information from the works listed in section 13 of *English genealogy: an introductory bibliography*. Emphasis here is placed on nineteenth-century directories. It should be noted that I have not, in general, listed directories which cover a large number of counties, although many of these have important Buckinghamshire content. The list which follows is in rough chronological order.

Post Office directory of Berkshire, Northamptonshire, Oxfordshire with Bedfordshire, Buckinghamshire and Huntingdonshire ... Kelly & Co., 1847-1939. 19 issues. Variously titled; also known as *Kelly's directory ...*; sometimes issued as a single county volume; sometimes in a volume with various other counties.

Musson & Craven's commercial directory of the county of Buckingham and the town of Windsor ... Nottingham: Stevenson & Co., 1853.

Dutton Allen & Co's directory & gazetteer of the counties of Oxon, Berks & Bucks ... Manchester: Dutton Allen & Co., 1863.

History, topography and directory of Buckinghamshire, Cambridgeshire and Hertfordshire ... Edward Cassey & Co., 1865.

J.G. Harrod & Co's royal county directory of Bedfordshire, Buckinghamshire, Berkshire and Oxfordshire. Norwich: Royal County Directory Offices, 1876.

Deacon's court guide gazetteer and royal blue book embracing the Western division of the County of Surrey, with Staines, Windsor, Eton, Slough, Maidenhead and their surrounding districts. 2nd ed. C.W. Deacon & Co., 1878.

Deacon's Berkshire, Buckinghamshire and Oxfordshire court guide and county blue book ... 2nd ed. Charles William Deacon, 1890.

Buckinghamshire and South Surrey district trades directory. Edinburgh: Town and County Directories, 1913-26. 2 issues.

Berkshire, Buckinghamshire and Oxfordshire directory. Walsall: Aubrey & Co., 1938-40. 4 vols.

Amersham

Hall's directory of Amersham, Chesham, Great Missenden and district, 1930-31. Reading: Ernest Hall & Co., 1930.

Aylesbury

Poulton's Aylesbury directory. Aylesbury: Poulton, [c.1880].

The Aylesbury directory and official handbook for the County of Bucks. Aylesbury: G.T. De Fraine, 1907-32. 10 issues. Continued by:

Kelly's directory of Aylesbury & neighbourhood, incorporating the Aylesbury Directory (G.T. De Fraine & Co. Ltd.). Kelly's Directories, 1936-48.

Chesham

Kelly's directory of Chesham and Amersham, including Chesham Bois, Great Missenden and Little Missenden ... Kelly's Directories, 1933-41. 6 issues.

Gerrard's Cross

Gerrard's Cross & Chalfont St.Peter directory ..., guide and diary. Gerrards Cross: Gerrards Cross and Chalfont St.Peter Volunteer Fire Brigade, 1917-21. 2 issues.

Binder's directory of Gerrards Cross and Chalfont St.Peter. Gerrards Cross: R. Binder, 1931-40. 3 issues.

Great Marlow

Marlow directory and almanack. Marlow: Marlow Printing Works, 1915.

Haddenham

McLAUGHLIN, EVE, ed. *Haddenham in 1909: directory of inhabitants.* Haddenham: Buckinghamshire Publications, 1993. From an old directory.

High Wycombe

The Wycombe and South Bucks almanack and directory for 1852. Wycombe: W. Butler, 1852.

A local guide and directory for the town of High Wycombe and its neighbourhood, including Beaconsfield, Missenden, Risborough, Marlow, Penn, Stockenchurch, and Wooburn ... High Wycombe: William Judson, 1875.

The High Wycombe directory, handbook and advertiser. Stenlake & Simpson, 1885.

Newport Pagnell

SIMPSON, JOSEPH. *History of the town of Newport Pagnell and its neighbourhood.* Newport Pagnell: Simpson & Son, 1868. Includes a directory.

Slough

Palmer's directory and year book for Slough and district, containing a list of the principal inhabitants, and a variety of useful local information. Slough: Palmers, 1908-9. 2 issues. Continued by:

Day's (late Palmer's) directory and year book for Slough and District, containing a list of the principal residents, and a variety of useful local information. Slough: I. Day, 1912-14. 3 issues.

Kelly's directory of Slough & neighbourhood, including Burnham, Farnham Royal & Stoke Poges ... Kelly's Directories, 1936-40. 3 issues.

Directories sometimes, usefully, include maps, which you will need to consult to identify particular places. Early maps reveal much about the way in which the landscape has changed in modern times. The original Ordnance Survey maps are particularly useful, and have been recently reprinted:

The old series Ordnance Survey maps of England and Wales ... vol.IV: Central England. Lympne Castle: Harry Margary, 1986.

Individual sheet maps of the first edition 1" Ordnance Survey maps have also recently been reprinted by the publishers David & Charles.

Two recent works include reproductions of historic maps:

SCOTT, VALERIE, & McLAUGHLIN, EVE. *Buckinghamshire.* County maps and histories series. Quiller Press, 1984.

WYATT, GORDON. *Maps of Bucks.* ed. Clive Birch. Buckingham: Barracuda Books, 1978.

A number of works provide lists of Buckinghamshire maps:

BUCKINGHAMSHIRE RECORD OFFICE *Catalogue of maps.* Occasional publication **3**. [Aylesbury]: the Office, 1961. Manuscript maps.

ELVEY, ELIZABETH MARY. *A handlist of Buckinghamshire estate maps.* B.R.S. lists and indexes **2**, 1963.

PRICE, URSULA. 'The maps of Buckinghamshire, 1574-1800', *R.o.B.* **15**, 1947, 107-33, 182-207 & 250-69.

For guidance on locating parishes within hundreds, see:

'Know your hundreds', *O.* **16**(4), 1992, 137-8; **17**(1), 1993, 27.

To identify obscure place-names, you will need to consult:

MAWER, A., & STENTON, F.M. *The place-names of Buckinghamshire.* English Place-Name Society **2**, 1925.

A few local maps giving the names of house owners and/or occupiers have recently been published in facsimile:

McLAUGHLIN, EVE, ed. *Aylesbury residents in 1806-1809.* Haddenham: Buckinghamshire Publications, 1993.

McLAUGHLIN, EVE, ed. *A map of Whaddon village, 1800.* Haddenham: Buckinghamshire Publications, 1992.

12. RELIGIOUS RECORDS

Religion played a much more important role in medieval society than it does today. Consequently, many of the sources essential to the genealogist are to be found in ecclesiastical rather than state archives—for example, parish registers, probate records, local government records, etc. Works on ecclesiastical sources are listed throughout this bibliography; this chapter concentrates on those topics which are primarily to do with the administration of the church. Buckinghamshire in the medieval period was a part of the Diocese of Lincoln. For interesting introductions to the 15-16th c. diocese, see:

BOWKER, MARGARET. *The secular clergy in the Diocese of Lincoln, 1495-1520.* Cambridge: C.U.P., 1968. Includes various lists of clergy.

BOWKER, MARGARET. *The Henrician Reformation in the Diocese of Lincoln: the Diocese of Lincoln under John Longland, 1521-1547.* Cambridge: C.U.P., 1981.

The most important ecclesiastical records of the medieval church are the bishops' registers, which record the general business of the diocese. The lists of ordinations and institutions they contain, together with the occasional will, are of particular value to genealogists. Published registers of the Diocese of Lincoln include:

PHILLIMORE, W.P.W., ed. *Rotuli Hugonis de Welles, episcopi Lincolniensis A.D. MCCIX-MCCXXXV.* 3 vols. Lincoln Record Society **3, 6** & **9.** Final vol. ed. F.N. Davis. Also published by Canterbury and York Society **1, 3** & **4.** Vol.3. includes institutions in the Buckingham Archdeaconry.

DAVIS, F.N., ed. *Rotuli Roberti Grosseteste, episcopi Lincolniensis, A.D. MCCXXXV-MCCLIII, necnon, Rotulus Henrici de Lexington, episcopi Lincolniensis A.D. MCCLIV-MCCLIX.* Lincoln Record Society **11,** 1914. Also published by Canterbury and York Society **10.**

DAVIS, F.N., et al, eds. *Rotulii Ricardi Gravesend, Episcopi Lincolniensis, A.D. MCCLVIII-MCCLXXIX.* Lincoln Record Society **20,** 1925. Also published by Canterbury and York Society **31.** Includes many Buckinghamshire institutions.

HILL, ROSALIND M.T., ed. *The rolls and register of Bishop Oliver Sutton, 1280-1299. vols.III-VII: Memoranda.* Lincoln Record Society **48, 52, 60, 64** & **69,** 1954-75.

ARCHER, MARGARET, ed. *The register of Bishop Philip Repingdon, 1405-1419.* 3 vols. Lincoln Record Society **57-8** & **75**, 1963-82.

See also:

LE NEVE, JOHN. *Fasti ecclesiae Anglicanae 1066-1300, III: Lincoln.* comp. Diana E. Greenway. Institute of Historical Research, 1977. Includes lists of the Archdeacons of Buckingham and various other dignitaries.

CLARK, ANDREW, ed. *Lincoln Diocese documents, 1450-1544.* Early English Text Society **149**. Kegan Paul, Trench, Trubner & Co., 1914.

THOMPSON, A. HAMILTON, ed. *Visitation of religious houses in the Diocese of Lincoln.* Lincoln Record Society **7**, **14** & **21**, 1914-29. Also published by Canterbury and York Society, vols. **17**, **24** & **33**. 15th c., includes information on founders.

THOMPSON, A. HAMILTON, ed. *Visitations in the Diocese of Lincoln, 1517-1531.* 3 vols. Lincoln Records Society **33**, **35** & **37**, 1940-44. Gives many names of Buckinghamshire clergy.

FOSTER, C.W., ed. *The registrum antiquissimum of the Cathedral church of Lincoln.* Lincoln Record Society **27-9**, 1931-5. Includes some Buckinghamshire documents.

RAGG, F.W. 'Fragment of folio ms. of Archdeaconry Courts of Buckinghamshire, 1491-1495', *R.o.B.* **11**, 1920-26, 27-47, 59-76, 145-56, 199-207 & 315-42.

HODGETT, G.A.J., ed. *The state of the ex-religious and former chantry priests in the Diocese of Lincoln, 1547-1574 from returns in the Exchequer.* Lincoln Record Society publications **53**, 1959. For the return from the Archdeaconry of Buckingham, see 96-100.

At the Reformation, the Archdeaconry of Buckingham became a part of the Diocese of Oxford. General works on the Diocese include:

TURNER, W.H. 'Ecclesiastical court books of the Diocese of Oxford', *Oxfordshire Architectural and Historical Society Proceedings* N.S. **3**, 1880, 130-39. General discussion of contents.

MARSHALL, WILLIAM M. 'Episcopal activity in the Hereford and Oxford dioceses, 1660-1760', *Midland history* **8**, 1983, 106-20. General discussion of ordinations, confirmations and visitations.

Works on the Archdeaconry of Buckingham are listed here in rough chronological order:

LEE, FREDERICK GEORGE. 'Institutions to Buckinghamshire benefices, A.D. 1556-1557', *R.o.B.* **6**, 1887, 168-9.

BRINKWORTH, E.R.C., ed. *Episcopal visitation book for the Archdeaconry of Buckingham, 1662.* B.R.S. **7**, 1947 (for 1943).

'The clergy of Buckinghamshire in 1689', *O.* **2**(1), 1978, 18-20. List of those who took the oath of allegiance.

PEMBERTON, W.A. 'Some notes on the court of the Archdeaconry of Buckingham in the eighteenth and early nineteenth centuries', *R.o.B.* **22**, 1980, 19-32. General discussion.

COCKS, ALFRED HENEAGE. *The church bells of Buckinghamshire: their inscriptions, founders, uses and traditions &c.* Jarrold & Sons, 1897. Many names of founders, donors, churchwardens, etc., etc.

LEGG, EDWARD, ed. *Buckinghamshire returns of the census of religious worship, 1851.* B.R.S. **27**, 1991. Lists all churches and chapels, with names of ministers, etc.

A number of works provide information relating to specific parishes:

Bledlow

YOUNG, ALISON. 'Bledlow, II: church and parsons', *R.o.B.* **17**(5), 1965, 367-85. Includes list of clergy, 12-19th c.

Chalfont St.Giles

PHIPPS, POWNOLL W. 'The church of St.Giles Chalfont', *R.o.B.* **6**, 1887, 83-105. Includes list of rectors, plus a few memorials and parish register extracts.

Datchet

BOND, SHEILA. 'The medieval building and repair of the chancels of Datchet, Iver, Langley and Wraysbury churches', *R.o.B.* **19**, 1971-4, 1-7. Extracts from 14th c. accounts.

Dinton

McLAUGHLIN, EVE. 'The Godly ones', *O.* **4**(3), 1980, 26. Confirmees at Dinton, 1806 and 1829, and at Princes Risborough, 1832.

Great Marlow

BUTLER, B.H. 'The Marlow tithes: the Tithe Commutation Act 1836 and the rectory of Great Marlow', *R.o.B.* **31**, 1989, 1-12.

Hughendon

DISRAELI, CONINGSBY. 'A Hughendon vicar and his perambulations', *R.o.B.* **11**, 1920-26, 174-85. Records of perambulations, 1714 and 1738, giving many names of parishioners.

Nonconformity

BROAD, JOHN, ed. *Buckinghamshire dissent and parish life, 1669-1712.* B.R.S. **28**, forthcoming.

Nonconformity *continued*

STELL, CHRISTOPHER. *Non-conformist chapels and meeting-houses: Buckinghamshire.* H.M.S.O., 1986. List, with brief descriptions including notes on monumental inscriptions.

McLAUGHLIN, EVE. 'Why come ye not to church?', *O.* 4(1), 1980, 27. Lists those accused of failing to attend church in Aylesbury, 1661.

PETHER, VERA. 'The protestors', *O.* 5(1), 1981, 27. Lists Petitioners against the Protestant Dissenters Ministers Bill, 1811, from Aylesbury.

Baptists

PETHER, VERA. 'The Dissenters' petitions: Baptists and others in 1811 and 1813', *O.* 4(4), 1980, 26. Gives names of Colnbrook Baptist petitioners to the House of Lords in 1811 and 1813.

COLLIE, A. 'The G[eneral] B[aptist] Association in Bucks: excerpts from the minute-book in the custody of Alderman Clarke, J.P., of Wycombe', *Transactions of the Baptist Historical Society* 4, 1914-15, 84-7, 173-84 & 214-8. 18th c., many names.

CHAMPION, L.G., ed. *The General Baptist Church of Berkhamstead, Chesham and Tring.* English Baptist records 1, Baptist Historical Society, 1905. Minute book; many names.

DELL, ALAN. 'The Baptists of Askett chapel', *O.* 4(3), 1980, 26-7. List of members, 1891.

LEGG, EDWARD. 'The restless Baptists of Fenny Stratford', *O.* 12(2), 1988, 62-3.

WHITLEY, W.T., ed. *The church books of Ford or Cuddington and Amersham in the county of Bucks.* Baptist Historical Society, 1912. 17-18th c., includes many names of members, with baptisms and burials, etc.

Congregationalists

SUMMERS, W.H. *History of the Congregational churches in the Berks, South Oxon and South Bucks Association, with notes on the earlier nonconformist history of the district.* Newbury: W.J. Blacket, 1905. Brief histories of many individual churches, giving names of ministers, etc.

Methodists

SUTCLIFFE, BARRY P., & CHURCH, DAVID. *200 years of Chiltern Methodism.* Ilkeston: Morleys, 1988. Includes lists of churches, memorials, etc.

Quakers

SNELL, BEATRICE SAXON, ed. *The minute book of the monthly meeting of the Society of Friends for the upperside of Buckinghamshire, 1669-1690. B.A.S., R.S.* 1, 1937.

LAKE, CHRISTOPHER. 'Quakerism in Buckinghamshire', *O.* 2(4), 1978, 15-18. General discussion.

LAKE, CHRISTOPHER. 'The Society of Friends and marriage', *O.* 9(3), 1985, 88-93. Includes list of Buckinghamshire Quakers, 1723.

ROSE, WALTER. *Haddenham Quaker history, 1660-1870.* ed. James Brodie and Audrey Brodie. Quaker historical manuscripts 1. Wellington, N.Z.: New Zealand Yearly Meeting of the Society of Friends, 1988. Includes list of burials, pedigree of Rose, 16-20th c., etc.

SUMMERS, W.H. *Memories of Jordans and the Chalfonts, and the early Friends in the Chiltern Hundreds.* Hedley Brothers, 1904. History of the meeting at Chalfont St.Peter and Chalfont St.Giles; includes many names.

Roman Catholics

'Action against Catholics in Buckinghamshire', in PETTI, ANTHONY G., ed. *Recusant documents from the Ellesmere manuscripts.* Catholic Record Society Publications (Records series) 60, 1968, 283-305. Many names, 1696.

13. ESTATE AND FAMILY PAPERS, etc.

A. GENERAL

The records of estate administration (deeds, leases, rentals, surveys, accounts, etc.) are a mine of information for the genealogist. Many of these records have been published in full or part, although far more lie untouched in the archives. A number of general collections of Buckinghamshire deeds are available; see:

J[ENKINS], J.G., ed. *A calendar of deeds and other records preserved in the muniment room at the Museum, Aylesbury. B.A.S., R.S.* **5**, 1941. Calendar of a part of the Buckinghamshire Archaeological Society's collection of deeds; includes over 1000 abstracts.

FOWLER, G. HERBERT, & JENKINS, J.G., eds. *Early Buckinghamshire charters. B.A.S., R.S.* **3**, 1939. Miscellaneous charters, including a number from Hartwell, East Claydon and Chilton.

GAMBIER-PARRY, T.R., ed. *A collection of charters relating to Goring, Streatley, and the neighbourhood, 1181-1546, preserved in the Bodleian Library, with a supplement.* Oxfordshire Record series **13-14**, 1931-2. Goring, Oxfordshire; Streatley, Berkshire. Includes some Buckinghamshire deeds, with various pedigrees.

Abstracts of deeds collected by a bookseller are published in two works:

'Palaeography, genealogy, and topography', *Topographical quarterly* **7**, 1938-9, 93-110.

'The value of old parchment documents in genealogical and topographical research', *Genealogists quarterly* **4**, 1935-6, 48-71.

For feet of fines (one of the major series of medieval deeds), see:

HUGHES, M.W., ed. *A calendar of the feet of fines for the County of Buckingham, 7 Richard I to 44 Henry III. B.A.S., R.S.* **4**, 1940.

TRAVERS, ANITA, ed. *A calendar of the feet of fines for Buckinghamshire, 1259-1307, with an appendix, 1179-1259.* B.R.S. **25**, 1989.

The process of enclosing land from open field resulted in the creation of many documents. Enclosure awards usually include complete lists of land owners and tenants, and are consequently invaluable for genealogists. Awards for Buckinghamshire are listed in:

TATE, W.E. *A handlist of Buckinghamshire enclosure acts and awards.* Aylesbury: Buckinghamshire County Council, 1946.

For a general discussion of enclosure, see:

TURNER, M. 'Enclosure commissioners and Buckinghamshire Parliamentary enclosure', *Agricultural History Review* **25**, 1977, 120-29.

The records of insurance companies provide many names of policy-holders. For Sun Fire Office and Royal Exchange Assurance Office policy-holders in Buckinghamshire, see:

McLAUGHLIN, EVE. *Bucks directory 1775-84.* Haddenham: Buckinghamshire Publications, 1993.

Many families have preserved deeds and papers relating to their estates and businesses. Published material from the archives of particular families, and relating to various parts of the county, include:

Cooper

FARNELL, MARY. 'The account book of William Cooper, millwright of Aylesbury', *R.o.B.* **24**, 1982, 118-24. Includes lists of clients and workmen in 1830s.

Grey

JACK, R.I., ed. *The Grey of Ruthin valor: the valor of the English lands of Edmund Grey, Earl of Kent, drawn up from the ministers' accounts of 1467-8.* Bedfordshire Historical Record Society **46**, 1965. Includes Buckinghamshire lands.

Lee

LEE, FREDERICK GEORGE. 'Deeds, documents, letters and papers relating to the Lees of Quarrendon', *R.o.B.* **4**, 1870, 189-93. Abstracts of 30 family documents.

Rede

SALTER, H.E., ed. *The Boarstall cartulary.* Oxford Historical Society **88**, 1930. Calendar of the private cartulary of Edmund Rede of Boarstall, drawn up in 1444. Includes his will, 1489.

Somerset, Dukes of

The manuscripts of the Duke of Somerset at Maiden Bradley, Wilts', in HISTORICAL MANUSCRIPTS COMMISSION *Fifteenth report, appendix, part VII.* C.8552. H.M.S.O., 1898, i-ix, 1-151. Mainly letters but also includes deeds relating to Buckinghamshire, Devon, Cornwall and Wiltshire, medieval-16th c.

B. ECCLESIASTICAL ESTATES AND CARTULARIES, etc.

In the medieval period, a great deal of property was owned by ecclesiastical institutions such as churches, monasteries, dioceses, etc.

Ecclesiastical and other corporate records have survived much better than those of private families; many are in print. Those relating to Buckinghamshire are listed here. One useful general source are the ecclesiastical glebe terriers, which provide evidences of the lands held by the incumbent in each parish. See:

BERESFORD, M.W. 'Glebe terriers and open-field Buckinghamshire', *R.o.B.* **15**, 1947, 283-98, & **16**(1), 1953-4, 5-28. Includes list of terriers, with transcript of one for Maids Moreton, 1707.

Aylesbury

LITTLE, A.G. 'Grey Friars of Aylesbury', *R.o.B.* **14**, 1941-6, 77-98. See also 185-6. Includes abstracts of many deeds.

Eton College

LYTE, H.C. MAXWELL. 'Report on the manuscripts of Eton College', in HISTORICAL MANUSCRIPTS COMMISSION *Ninth report ...* C.3773. H.M.S.O., 1883, 349-58. Medieval deeds; Buckinghamshire and various other counties.

Luffield Priory

ELVEY, G.R., ed. *Luffield Priory charters.* B.R.S. **15** & **18**, 1968-75. Also published as Northamptonshire Record Society publications **22** & **26**. Mainly relating to Luffield, Shalstone, Evershaw and Thornborough, Buckinghamshire, and Silverstone and Whittlebury, Northamptonshire.

Missenden Abbey

JENKINS, J.G., ed. *The cartulary of Missenden Abbey.* 3 vols. *B.A.S., R.S.* **2**. B.R.S. **10** & **12**, 1938-62. The third vol. also published by the HISTORICAL MANUSCRIPTS COMMISSION as *Joint Publication* **1**. Many charters; also includes descent of the fee of Wendover to the mid-13th c., and pedigree of Hampden, 12-13th c.

Notley Abbey

JENKINS, J.G. 'The lost cartulary of Nutley Abbey', *Huntingdon Library quarterly* **17**, 1953-4, 379-96. Includes abstracts of 60 deeds.

Oseney Abbey

POSTLES, DAVID. 'The manorial accounts of Oseney Abbey, 1274-1348', *Archives* **14**(62), 1979, 75-80. General discussion; the Abbey had estates in Oxfordshire and Buckinghamshire.

SALTER, H.E., ed. *Cartulary of Oseney Abbey.* 6 vols. Oxford Historical Society **89-91**, **97-8** & **101**, 1929-36. v.97, and especially v.98, has much Buckinghamshire material.

Oxford University. New College

STEER, FRANCIS W. *The archives of New College, Oxford: a catalogue.* Phillimore, 1974. Includes an extensive listing of Buckinghamshire estate papers. See also:

HOBSON, T.F. *A catalogue of manorial documents preserved in the muniment room of New College, Oxford.* Manorial Society publications **16**, 1929. Lists many documents from Akeley, Hardwick, Horwood, Newton Longville, Raddive, and Tingewick; also various other counties.

'The annual progress of New College by Michael Woodward, warden, 1659-1675', *R.o.B.* **13**, 1934-40, 77-137. In Buckinghamshire.

Snelshall Priory

JENKINS, J.G., ed. *The cartulary of Snelshall Priory.* B.R.S. **9**, 1952. Abstract of 216 deeds.

Tickford Priory

FOWLER, G. HERBERT. 'Some early instruments of Tickford Priory', *R.o.B.* **11**, 1920-26, 225-32. 12th c. charters.

C. *LOCAL ESTATE RECORDS*

Many estate papers relating to particular places are in print; these are listed here, together with a few works based upon local estate records.

Amersham

'Amersham in the time of William and Mary', *R.o.B.* **13**, 1934-40, 208-23. Extracts from a rent roll, with list of tenants.

Aylesbury

PARKER, JOHN. 'The manor of Aylesbury', *Archaeologia* **50**(1), 1887, 81-103. Includes court roll, c.1500, with many names; also medieval pedigree showing descent of the manor through Boteler and Bullen.

Bassetsbury

16th and 17th century list of names and descriptions of copyhold messages &c., in Bassetsbury Manor. Mini-publication **1**. High Wycombe: High Wycombe History Society, 1969.

Bletchley

See Fenny Stratford

Burnham

N., J.G. 'Charters relating to the Abbey of Burnham, Co.Buckingham', *Collectanea topographica et genealogica* **8**, 1843, 120-31.

Burnham *continued*

WILLIAMS, WILLIAM H., ed. *Burnham (Bucks)*
church deeds: facsimiles of feoffments of land &
other ancient documents relating to the parish
church of St.Peter, Burnham, Buckinghamshire,
with transcriptions & translations of the
originals. Artists Press, 1913. Mainly medieval
deeds, but also some accounts, etc.

Chalfont St.Peter

BENNELL, JOHN E.G. 'The manor of the Vicarage of
Chalfont St.Peter', *R.o.B.* **17**(5), 1965, 392-402.
Includes rental, 1683.

ELVEY, ELIZABETH. 'The Abbot of Missenden's
estates in Chalfont St.Peter', *R.o.B.* **17**(1), 1961,
20-40. Includes names of tenants from a 1333
survey.

Claydon

ELVEY, G.R. 'Medieval charters at Claydon House',
R.o.B. **17**(2), 1962, 192-5. General discussion of
Claydon charters.

Codicote

RODEN, DAVID. 'Inheritance customs and
succession to land in the Chiltern Hills in the
13th and early 14th centuries', *Journal of*
British Studies **7**(1), 1967, 1-9. Based on
Codicote manorial records.

Crendon

B., W.H. 'The customs of the manor of Crendon, in
Buckinghamshire, 1558', *Collectanea*
topographica et genealogica **5**, 1838, 200-1.
Includes names of tenants.

Edlesborough

BIRCH, W. DE GRAY. 'Original documents in the
possession of T.F. Halsey, esq., M.P.', *Journal*
of the British Archaeological Association **34**,
1878, 391-6. Medieval deeds, mainly relating to
Buckinghamshire, especially Edlesborough.

Fawley

BAYLEY, W. D'OYLY. 'Ancient deeds, Bucks and
Oxon', *Topographer and Genealogist* **2**, 1853,
340-44. Includes deeds relating to Fawley and
Hambledon.

Fenny Stratford

BRADBROOK, W. 'Manor court rolls of Fenny
Stratford and Etone (Bletchley)', *R.o.B.* **11**,
1920-26, 289-314. 14th c. General discussion
with list of surnames occurring.

Frieth

RAY, MARY. 'Frieth residents, 1890', *O.* **8**(2), 1984,
54. List of names on a map drawn 1890.

Haddenham

'Haddenham copyholders, May 1785', *Bucks*
ancestor **1**(1), 1992, 11. List.

Hambledon

See Fawley

Hartwell

'Hartwell deeds', *R.o.B.* **13**, 1934-40, 447-9. Brief
calendar of a collection of 900 deeds.

Hillesden

'Hillesden account book, 1661-1667', *R.o.B.* **11**,
1920-26, 135-144, 186-98 & 244-55. Estate
account book; many names.

Latimer

PALMER, PEGGY. 'Some findings from the Latimer
manorial court book, 1745-1829', *Chess Valley*,
1988, 25-7. Includes brief extracts.

Newton Longville

SALTER, H.E., ed. *Newington Longville charters.*
Oxfordshire Record Series **3**. 1921. 12-15th c.

Pitstone

HANLEY, H.A. 'The inclosure of Pitstone Common
Wood in 1612', *R.o.B.* **29**, 1987, 175-204. Lists
claimants to rights in the wood, 1607-1610/11,
signatories of 1612 inclosure agreement, etc.

Upton

DENINGTON, R.F. 'The Upton cum Chalvey
inclosure award', *News Bulletin of the Middle*
Thames Archaeological and Historical Society
3(19), 1974, 146-51. Lists landowners.

Waddesdon

BALLARD, A. 'Notes on the court rolls of the
rectorial manor at Waddesdon', *R.o.B.* **10**, 1916,
98-100. Mainly 17th c.

Water Eaton

HOLLIS, EDWIN. 'Farm accounts, late 14th century',
R.o.B. **12**, 1927-33, 165-92. From Water Eaton;
transcript giving names.

Wedon Hill

'The Shardeloes muniments, II: Wedon Hill
Manor, 1629-1745', *R.o.B.* **14**, 1941-6, 210-35.
Extracts from rent rolls.

Winslow

'A court roll of Winslow', *R.o.B.* **13**, 1934-40, 12-
24. 1671; includes list of personal names in roll.

'The building of Winslow Hall', *R.o.B.* **11**, 1920-
26, 406-29. Includes extracts from accounts, 17-
18th c., with many names of labourers, etc.

Wooburn

RAY, MARY. 'Wooburn residents, 1803', *O.* **8**(2), 1984, 54. Names from an enclosure plan.

D. *MANORIAL DESCENTS, etc.*

Many historians have worked out the descent of manors and other property. A number of general histories including such descents are listed in section 1. Descents of particular properties are listed here.

Biddlesden Abbey

ROUNDELL, H. 'Biddlesden Abbey and its lands', *R.o.B.* **1**, 1858, 277-87 & **2**, 1863, 34-40 & 75-80. Traces medieval descents.

Bledlow

YOUNG, ALISON. 'Bledlow, I: land tenures and the three-field system', *R.o.B.* **17**(4), 1964, 266-85. Includes descents of properties.

Burnham

BROADBENT, JOHN D. 'Survey of two properties in High Street, Burnham', *R.o.B.* **17**(2), 1962, 197-201. Includes descent of the property, 1560-1913.

Calverton

ELWES, DUDLEY GEORGE CARY. 'Notes on Calverton manor, County Buckingham', *R.o.B.* **5**, 1878, 120-32. Traces descent.

Chequers

JENKINS, JOHN GILBERT. *Chequers: a history of the Prime Minister's home.* Oxford: Pergamon Press, 1967. Traces descent; includes folded pedigree of the lords of Wolverton and of the Hawtrey family, medieval-17th c.

Coleshill

TRENCH, JOHN CHENEVIX. 'The houses of Coleshill—the social anatomy of a seventeenth century village', *R.o.B.* **25**, 1983, 61-109. Attempts to trace occupants of each home.

Great Hampden

PARKER, JOHN. 'The lords of Great Hampden manor', *R.o.B.* **6**, 1887, 144-53. Medieval-18th c.

Hartwell

SMYTH, W.H. *Aedes Hartwellianae, or, notices of the manor and mansion of Hartwell.* John Bowyer Nichols and Son, 1851. Includes chapter on the successive lords of the manor.

Hedsor

BOSTON, LORD 'Notes on the history of the manor and church of Hedsor', *R.o.B.* **8**, 1903, 487-516. Manorial descent, medieval, with list of rectors, 1201-1880.

Hitcham

PACKE, A.H., & BROADBENT, J.D. 'Hitcham old barn', *R.o.B.* **18**(4), 1969, 313-7. Historical note traces descent of the manor of Hitcham.

Huntercombe

THOMAS, G.F. *A history of Huntercombe manor.* [ ]: Buckinghamshire Education Committee, 1969. Includes descent of the manor.

Iselhampstead Latimer

'Latimer and Nevill, Barons Latimer, in connection with the manor of Iselhampsted Latimer, Bucks., pedigree showing descent from Reinbudcurt, Foliot, Ledet and Braibroke; continued through Willoughby and Greville to Verney, Baron Willoughby de Broke and through Danvers and Walmesley to Osborne, Viscount Latimer, Duke of Leeds, etc.', *R.o.B.* **6**, 1887, 48-54. 12-18th c.

RUTTON, WILLIAM LOFTIE. 'Notes in reference to the family of Foliot, and to the Latimer and Nevill, Barons Latimer, etc., in connection with the manor of Iselhampsted-Latimer in Buckinghamshire', *R.o.B.* **6**, 1887, 55-71. See also 170-73. Medieval.

14. NATIONAL, COUNTY AND LOCAL ADMINISTRATION

A. NATIONAL AND COUNTY

Official lists of names, such as tax lists and census schedules, have already been discussed. There are, however, many other records of central and local government which provide useful information. For the leading officers of county administration—the sheriffs and lords lieutenants—see:

HANLEY, H.A. *The Buckinghamshire sheriffs.* [Aylesbury]: Buckinghamshire Record Office, 1992.

VINEY, ELLIOTT. *The sheriffs of Buckinghamshire from the eleventh century to the present day.* Aylesbury: Hazell Watson & Viney, 1965.

VINEY, ELLIOTT. 'The Buckinghamshire lieutenancy', *R.o.B.* **19**, 1971-4, 113-40. Brief biographies of lords lieutenants.

Published medieval records include (in chronological order):

FOWLER, G. HERBERT, & HUGHES, MICHAEL W., eds. *A calendar of the pipe rolls of the reign of Richard I for Buckinghamshire and Bedfordshire, 1189-1199.* Publications of the Bedfordshire Historical Record Society **7**, 1923.

JENKINS, J.G., ed. *Calendar of the roll of the Justices on Eyre, 1227. B.A.S., R.S.* **6**, 1945.

FOWLER, G. HERBERT, ed. *Rolls from the office of the sheriff of Beds and Bucks, 1332-1334.* Quarto memoirs of the Bedfordshire Historical Record Society **3**, 1929.

JENKINS, J.G. 'An early coroner's roll for Buckinghamshire', *R.o.B.* **13**, 1934-40, 163-85. 1377-90.

'Dick Crookback's men', *O.* **9**(4), 1985, 130-36. Includes pedigree of Hampden, 15th c., with list of Buckinghamshire manors held by supporters of the Yorkist and Lancastrian contenders for the throne.

LEADAM, I.S., ed. *The Domesday of inclosures, 1517-1518: being the extant returns to Chancery for Berks, Bucks, Cheshire, Essex, Leicestershire, Lincolnshire, Northants and Warwickshire, by the Commissioners of Inclosures in 1517, and for Bedfordshire in 1518, together with Dugdale's ms. notes of the Warwickshire inquisitions in 1517, 1518 and 1549.* 2 vols. Longmans Green & Co., 1897. Names many landlords.

From the seventeenth century, the records of Quarter Sessions become important. These have been fully calendared in:

LE HARDY, WILLIAM, ed. *County of Buckingham: calendar to the sessions records.* 8 vols. Aylesbury: Clerk to the Peace, 1933- (vols.1-3 are in a different format to vols.4-8, and may be shelved separately; vol.8 is in typescript but not yet published). Contents: v.1. 1678 to 1694. v.2. 1694 to 1705. v.3. 1705 to 1712 and appendix 1647. v.4. 1712-1718 and appendix 1703-1716. v.5. 1718-1724. v.6. List of persons who took oaths of allegiance, etc., and Quakers who affirmed, 1723-24; register of estates of Roman Catholics, 1717-48. v.7. 1724-1730. v.8. 1730-33; addenda 1663-1720.

See also:

JENKINS, DEBORAH. 'Quarter Sessions records', *O.* **7**(4), 1983, 110-13.

ELAND, G., ed. *Papers from an iron chest at Doddershall, Bucks.* Aylesbury: G.T. De Fraine & Co., 1937. Papers of the Pigott family, 16-17th c., mainly concerning the administration of the county.

VEYSEY, GEOFFREY. 'A justice's diary', *R.o.B.* **17**(2), 1962, 182-8. Extracts from diary of Sir Roger Hill, late 17th c., describing duties as a J.P. Many names.

Many references to local people at the time of the Great Rebellion are contained in:

LUKE, SIR SAMUEL. *The letter books of Sir Samuel Luke, 1644-45, Parliamentary governor of Newport Pagnell.* ed. H.G. Tibbutt. Historical Manuscripts Commission joint publication **4**. H.M.S.O., 1963. Also published as Bedfordshire Historical Record Society **42**.

For biographical notes on leading Parliamentarians, see:

BANNARD, H.E. 'The Berkshire, Buckinghamshire and Oxfordshire committees of 1642-1646', *B.B.O.A.J.* **31**(2), 1927, 173-92.

The nineteenth century was the great age of reform. Charities were an important target for the reformers, and the inquiries of the Charity Commissioners resulted in the publication of voluminous tomes of information, which include abstracts of many deeds, wills, and other estate documents. It is impossible to cite here everything relating to Buckinghamshire which is to be found amongst their reports; see, however:

CHARITY COMMISSIONERS *The reports of the Commissioners appointed in pursuance of various acts of Parliament to enquire concerning charities in England and Wales relating to the County of Buckingham, 1819-1837.* Henry Gray, [1837]. Reprinted from the Parliamentary papers.

Abstract of returns of charitable donations for poor persons in the County of Bucks. Aylesbury: T.W. Faulkner, 1820. Includes lists of donors and of persons 'in whom now vested'.

B. PAROCHIAL AND BOROUGH ADMINISTRATION

The records of parochial government—the accounts of churchwardens, overseers, and other parish officers, rate assessments, settlement papers, etc.—contain much information of genealogical value. Many extracts and transcripts for Buckinghamshire have been published, and are listed here.

Amersham

LEE, FREDERICK GEORGE. 'Amersham churchwardens' accounts', *R.o.B.* **7**, 1897, 43-51. 16-17th c. extracts.

'Amondesham als Amersham in com. Bucks: an assessm't made ... 1703 ... for ... the releife of the poor of the said parish ...', *Fragmenta Genealogica* **5**, 1900, 87-91.

Aston Abbots

BRADBROOK, WILLIAM. 'Aston Abbots: parish account book', *R.o.B.* **10**, 1916, 34-50. Extracts, 16-18th c.

Aylesbury

ELVEY, ELIZABETH M. 'Aylesbury in the fifteenth century: a bailiff's notebook', *R.o.B.* **17**(5), 1965, 321-35. Includes extracts, with many names.

Bledlow

QUICK, B.O., ed. *Bledlow charity book 1720-1830.* Haddenham: Buckinghamshire Publications, 1993. Transcript; names recipients.

'From Bledlow to the mills: pauper migration', *O.* **7**(3), 1982, 76-9. Discusses a petition of 1834 signed by 32 Bledlow paupers.

Chalfont St.Giles

EDMONDS, GEOFFREY C. 'Accounts of eighteenth-century overseers of the poor of Chalfont St.Giles', *R.o.B.* **18**(1), 1966, 3-23.

Chearsley

HOOTON, TED. 'The inhabitants of Chearsley, 1801-1955', *O.* **9**(3), 1985, 113-4. Description of a project to record all inhabitants.

Chesham

THOMAS, ANNA M., FOXELL, SHIRLEY, & BAINES, ARNOLD H.J. 'The Weedon charity in Chesham', *R.o.B.* **19**, 1971-4, 302-16. General discussion.

GARRETT-PEGG, J.W. 'Richard Bowle's book', *R.o.B.* **9**, 1909, 329-48 & 393-414; **10**, 1916, 1-18. Records the restoration of Chesham church, 1606; includes a rate assessment, seating plan (listing all inhabitants), accounts, etc.

Cholesbury

BAINES, ARNOLD. 'The vestry of Cholesbury, 1820-1894', *R.o.B.* **17**(1), 1961, 57-81. Based on vestry books.

Clifton Reynes

BRADBROOK, WILLIAM. 'Clifton Reynes parish account book', *R.o.B.* **11**, 1920-26, 91-102. Brief extracts, 1665-1723.

Haddenham

'Haddenham during the Civil War', *R.o.B.* **12**, 1927-33, 73-80. Transcript of accounts, 1643, with many names.

Hawridge

BAINES, ARNOLD H.J. 'The select vestry of Hawridge', *R.o.B.* **18**(1), 1966, 34-42. 19th c., based on vestry book.

High Wycombe

DOWNS, R.S. 'The parish church of High Wycombe (third notice): extracts from the churchwardens' and overseers accounts', *R.o.B.* **8**, 1903, 55-87.

GREAVES, R.W., ed. *The first ledger book of High Wycombe.* B.R.S. **11**, 1956. 14-18th c.

NEWALL, W.A., ed. *The ledger book of the Corporation of Chepping Wycombe in Com. Bucks, 1684-1770.* [High Wycombe]: High Wycombe History Society, 1965.

RILEY, HENRY THOMAS. 'The borough of High Wycombe, or Chipping Wycombe, Bucks', in HISTORICAL MANUSCRIPTS COMMISSION *Fifth report ...* C.1432. H.M.S.O., 1876, 554-64.

Iver

McLAUGHLIN, EVE, ed. *Iver settlement papers 1699-1845.* 2nd ed. Haddenham: Buckinghamshire Publications, 1993.

Medmenham

PLAISTEAD, ARTHUR H. *The manor and parish records of Medmenham, Buckinghamshire.* Longmans Green & Co., 1925. Includes a descent of the manor, lists of wills, incumbents, etc.

Newport Pagnell

McLAUGHLIN, EVE, ed. *Newport Pagnell settlement papers 1660-1837.* 2nd ed. Haddenham: Buckinghamshire Publications, 1993.

Newton Longville

BRADBROOK, W. 'Newton Longville parish books', *R.o.B.* **11**, 1920-26, 1-10. Includes rate assessment, 1696, etc.

Pitstone

ELVEY, ELIZABETH, FARNELL, MARY, & KEMP, ANDREW, eds. *The book of accounts for the parish of Pitstone, 1604-25*. Pitstone: Pitstone Church Committee, 1979.

Quainton

'Churchwardens' accounts of Quainton', *R.o.B.* **12**, 1927-33, 29-46. Extracts, 1668-1735.

'Churchwardens' accounts', *O.* **16**(3), 1992, 113-5. Includes list of apprentices from Quainton, 18th c.

McLAUGHLIN, EVE, ed. *Quainton settlement papers*. Haddenham: Buckinghamshire Publications, 1993. Includes list of those apprenticed by the Pigott and Saye and Sele charities.

Stoke Poges

McLAUGHLIN, EVE, ed. *Stoke Poges settlement papers 1700-1856*. 2nd ed. Haddenham: Buckinghamshire Publications, 1993.

Thornborough

McLAUGHLIN, E. 'The inhabitants of Thornborough', *O.* **4**(1), 1980, 23-4. List of pewholders, 1720, with list of property owners, 1723.

Tingewick

'Tingewick allotments', *O.* **15**(1), 1991, 26. List of allotment holders, 1833.

Wendover

'A parish apprentice indenture', *O.* **7**(2), 1983, 42. Includes brief extracts from Wendover apprenticeship indentures.

Wing

LOYD, L.H. 'The churchwardens' accounts of Wing, Co.Bucks', *Journal of the British Archaeological Association* **44**, 1888, 51-9. 16th c.

OUVRY, FREDERIC. *Extracts from the churchwardens' accounts of Wing in the County of Buckingham*. J.B. Nichols & Son, 1856. Reprinted from *Archaeologia* **36**(2), 1856, 219-41.

WOODMAN, A. VERE. 'The accounts of the churchwardens of Wing', *R.o.B.* **16**(5), 1960, 307-29. 16th c. extracts.

Wooburn

McLAUGHLIN, EVE, ed. *Wooburn settlement papers*. Haddenham: Buckinghamshire Publications, 1993.

STAFF, PAT. 'So good to the poor', *O.* **10**(2), 1986, 53-7. Discussion of records in the Wooburn parish chest.

15. EDUCATIONAL RECORDS

The records of schools can provide the genealogist with much information. Many records of schools—including school ledgers, log books, minute books, etc.—have been lodged with Buckinghamshire Record Office, and are listed in:

BUCKINGHAMSHIRE RECORD OFFICE *Education records*. Occasional publications **1**. Aylesbury: the Office, 1961.

School log books are particularly useful. A general discussion of their value is provided by:

GROF, LASZLO. 'Log books: a mirror on life', *O.* **12**(4), 1988, 25-7. Includes Buckinghamshire list, 19th c.

Histories and registers of a number of schools are available. The following brief listing is not comprehensive; rather, it seeks to identify those works which have a particular genealogical value.

Amersham

TREADGOLD, F.R. *Challoners, 1624-1974: the story of Dr. Challoner's Grammar School, Amersham.* Luton: Leagrave Press, 1974. Includes pedigree of Chaloner, 16-17th c., list of headmasters, etc.

Eton College

Eton is undoubtedly the most well known public school in England today, and its students are drawn from throughout the country—and, indeed, the world. It was not always so; in its early years, Eton's catchment area was much smaller, and its social composition much less aristocratic than it became in the nineteenth century. There are many histories of the school: they include:

HOLLIS, CHRISTOPHER. *Eton: a history.* Hollis & Carter, 1960. Includes a useful bibliography.

HUSSEY, CHRISTOPHER. *Eton College, with an account of Oppidan Eton.* 4th ed. Country Life, 1952. Includes list of boarding house tenants.

LYTE, H.C. MAXWELL. *A history of Eton College (1440-1910).* 4th ed. Macmillan, 1911.

Many lists of Eton pupils, staff, etc. have been published. See (in rough chronological order):

Registrum Regale: a list of I the Provosts of Eton II the Provosts of King's College, Cambridge III the Fellows of Eton IV Alumni Etonensis, in annual succession from Eton to Kings College, from ... 1441 to 1847, with illustrative and biographical notes. Eton: Edward Pote Williams, 1847.

STERRY, WASEY. *The Eton College Register, 1441-1698, alphabetically arranged and edited with biographical notes.* Eton: Spottiswoode Ballantyre & Co., 1943.

STERRY, WASEY. *A list of Eton commensals, 1563-1647.* Eton College: Spottiswoode & Co., 1904.

AUSTEN-LEIGH, R.A., ed. *A list of Eton Collegers, 1661-1790.* Eton: Spottiswoode & Co., 1905.

AUSTEN-LEIGH, R.A., ed. *Eton College lists, 1678-1790.* Eton College: Spottiswoode & Co., 1907.

AUSTEN-LEIGH, RICHARD ARTHUR. *The Eton College register, 1698-1752, arranged alphabetically and edited with biographical notes.* Eton: Spottiswoode Ballantyne & Co., 1927. Continued by his *The Eton College register, 1753-1790 ...* Eton: Spottiswoode Ballantyne & Co., 1921.

AUSTEN-LEIGH, R.A. *A list of Eton College in 1771.* Eton: College Press, 1903. Includes pedigrees of Hawtrey, Sleech, Thackeray, Sumner, Roberts, Drury and Heath, 17-19th c.

STAPYLTON, H.E.C. *The Eton School lists, from 1791 to 1850 (every third year after 1793), with notes.* 2nd ed. E.P. Williams, 1864. Includes lists of provosts and fellows, masters, cricket elevens and boat's crews.

The Eton register. 8 vols. Eton: Spottiswoode & Co., for the Old Etonian Association, 1903-32. Covers 1841-1919; includes brief biographies.

STAPYLTON, H.E.C. *Second series of Eton school lists, comprising the years between 1853 and 1892, with notes and index.* Eton: R. Ingalton Drake, 1900.

The Eton register, being a continuation of Stapylton's Eton school lists, 1893-1899. Eton: Spottiswoode & Co., 1901.

The old public school-boys who's who series: Eton. St.James Press, 1933.

VAUGHAN, E.L. *List of Etonians who fought in the Great War 1914-1919.* P. Lee Warner for Eton College, 1921.

List of Etonians who fought in the World War 1939-1945. Eton: [Eton College?], 1950.

Many other titles of potential interest are listed in:

HARCOURT, L.V. *An Eton bibliography.* New ed. Arthur L. Humphreys, 1902.

High Wycombe

ASHFORD, L.J., & HAWORTH, C.M. *The history of the Royal Grammar School, High Wycombe, 1562 to 1962.* High Wycombe: the Governors, 1962. Includes lists of 20th c. assistant masters and winners of awards; also many other names in passing.

BURNE, A.T. *Wycombe Abbey School register, 1896-1910 (revised to 1914), with alphabetical index.* [ ], 1914.

Wavendon

COLE, JEAN. 'Pupils at Wavendon End school, 19th century (n.d.)', *O.* **10**(2), 1986, 68. List.

FAMILY NAME INDEX

PLACE NAME INDEX

AUTHOR INDEX

Abbott, E. 36
Adkins, B. 17, 19, 24
Allaby, M. 11
Allaby, S. 11
Andrews, A. 35
Archer, M. 40
Ashford, L.J. 49
Ashford, P. 14
Austen-Leigh, R.A. 49
Ayto, E.G. 14

B., W.H. 44
Badham, S. 31
Baines, A. 47
Baldwin, R.T. 35
Bale, R.F. 25, 27, 28
Ballard, A. 44
Bannard, H.E. 46
Bannerman, W.B. 26-28
Barnard, E.A.B. 20
Barratt, D.M. 29
Bartlett, E. 23
Bayley, W.D. 44
Beaconsfield and District Historical
    Society 24
Beckett, I.F.W. 8, 35
Bedford, A.M. 31
Bennell, J.E.G. 33, 44
Beresford, M.W. 43
Berrill, N.J. 34
Berry, G. 15
Berry, W. 12
Bicknell, A.S. 23
Birch, C. 38
Birch, W. De G. 44
Black, W.H. 8
Blair, J. 31
Bletchley Archaeological and
    Historical Society 24, 26-7
Bloom, J.H. 16, 20
Blundell, J.H. 16
Boddington, R.S. 16, 32
Bond, S. 40
Bonsey, C.G. 34
Boodle, J.A. 31
Boston, Lord 45
Bowker, M. 39
Bradbrook, W. 11, 16, 24-29, 31-
    33, 44, 47, 48

Briden, E.J. 16
Brinkworth, E.R.C. 40
Broad, J. 22, 40
Broadbent, J.D. 45
Brodie, A. 41
Brodie, J. 41
Brown, O.F. 22
Browne, A.L. 30
Bruce, J. 22
Buckinghamshire Family History
    Society 13
Buckinghamshire Record Office 9,
    10, 20, 38
Bunce, F.M. 11
Burne, A.T. 49
Burrows, M. 16
Butler, B.H. 40

Carr-Gomm, F. 9, 34
Carter, W.F. 18
Chambers, J. 14
Champion, L.G. 41
Charity Commissioners 46
Charlton, S. 10
Chess Valley Archaeological and
    Historical Society 25, 30
Chester, J.L. 16
Cheyne, E. 29
Chibnall, A.C. 7, 9, 34, 35
Chorlton, N. 35
Church, D. 41
Clark, A. 40
Clark, C.F. 25
Clark, E. 21
Clark-Maxwell, W.G. 12
Clarke, H.A. 31
Clear, A. 24, 30
Coales, J. 33
Cocks, A.H. 26, 32, 33, 40
Cokayne, G.E. 20
Coldham, P.W. 13
Cole, J. 49
Cole, W. 9, 25
Coleman, Mr 16
Collie, A. 41
Collins, Sir W.J. 22
Commonwealth War Graves
    Commission 31
Coppock, J.C. 12

Cornwall, J. 7, 8, 10, 30
Craik, A. 19
Crisp, F.A. 29
Croke, A., Sir 17
Crowton, P. 36
Cullum, G.M.G. 23

Dashwood, Sir F. 17
Davies, L.W. 13, 14, 35
Davis, F.N. 39
Davis, R. 21
Dawson-Smith, C.C. 28
Dayrell, E. 17
De Rothschild, Mrs J. 21
Deane, M. 18
Delafield, J.R. 18
Dell, A. 9, 14, 18, 19, 32, 41
Denington, R.F. 44
Deverill, P. 18
Dickett, G.F., Sir 18
Dickson, R.B. 28
Disraeli, C. 40
Downs, R.S. 26, 32, 47
Duncombe, R.F. 18
Dunlop, J.R. 33

E., D.C. 20
E., E.M. 24
Ebblewhite, E.A. 26
Edmonds, G.C. 47
Eland, G. 11, 21, 23, 46
Elliston, R.J. 14
Elvey, E. 23, 29, 38, 44, 47, 48
Elvey, G. 23, 43, 44
Elwes, D.G.C. 25, 45
Esdaile, K.A. 31
Eustace, D.W. 18
Evans, H.F.O. 32, 34

Fairfax-Lucy, A. 20
Farnell, M. 42, 48
Fell, S.G. 17
Ferrers, C.S.F. 18
Finch, J. 18
Ford, J.C. 19
Foster, C.W. 40
Fowler, G.H. 42, 43, 46
Foxell, S. 47
French, J. 36